The Seventh Wife

A NOVEL

Francile McCottry

The Seventh Wife
Published by Angel Wing Enterprise
P.O. Box 25
Cedar Hill, Texas 75106-0025
Email: Fmccottry@yahoo.com

The characters and events in this novel are fictional. However, portions of this novel are based on actual events.

ISBN- 0971137684
ISBN-978-0-9711376-8-4

Copyright ©2015 by Francile Curry McCottry
All rights reserved. No parts of this book may be reproduced or transmitted in any form without the written permission in writing from the author.

Published in the United States of America by Angel Wing Enterprise.

Library of Congress Cataloging-in Publication Data is on file with the Library of Congress.

Printed in the United States of America
2015-First edition.

The Seventh Wife

The quest for love will sometimes navigate you into many horizons, in which you will suffer numerous heartaches, pain, and tragedies.

Yet, somehow we manage to survive these dilemmas finding the strength to continue moving forward with the hope of obtaining the emotional fulfillment of love.

After all, love is the ultimate expression of God, and the adoration of God's love that is expressed in human relationships.

Francile Curry

There are three things that will endure-faith, hope, and love-and the greatest of these is love.

I Corinthians 13:13

Dedication

For my husband Alvin (Brother Al) Leon McCottry.
Thank you so much for your love, and support.
Love you

CHAPTER 1

Camp Evans, Vietnam, January 1968

It was the early morning hours after suffering a fierce overnight battle in a place called "Happy Valley" when Private Barker, a twenty year old from Barksdale, Arizona, rushed into the camp of First Sergeant Richard McWilliams. "Sir, here are the causality reports from last night's engagement. Major Carter's orders are to type the report quickly and forward it over to the Pentagon." Fatigued, dirty, and bloody from the overnight battle and with no time to spare, Barker handed the sergeant the thick blood stained report. He then turned immediately and proceeded to make his way from the tent, but McWilliams quickly suggested that the weary young soldier sit awhile.

"No time to spare sir, I'm needed back at the camp. When you look at that report, you will see why I gotta get back to my camp. We lost most of our men last night! The 350-man ambush force was divided with two companies dug in. The enemy's plan to hit the front and the rear of our convoy failed but we still lost many of our men. We had to fight like hell to stay afloat until help arrived."

Slowly flipping through the pages of the report, fury and rage began to consume Sergeant McWilliams's face. His eyes were fixed on several familiar names. Suddenly, he let out a loud frustrated scream. "Damn! When is Johnson going to get us out of this God forsaken hellhole? This list is filled with the names of young boys who have given their lives for nothing!

Each time I look at the list I explode with anger! My prayer is for this nightmare to be over soon so we can go back to the states and reunite with our families."

"Sir, do you have family back home?" The young soldier's voice reaped with sincerity.

"Yep, I have a beautiful wife, two beautiful daughters, and my son, Richard Jr., who's six months old. They're all anxiously waiting for me back home in Fort Collins, Colorado. Returning home to my family will be like heaven on earth. I can't wait to see their beautiful faces. Do you have family back in the States?"

"No sir, I ain't married and I don't have any kids. It was just me and my old man but he died a few years ago. The Army is all I got, sir. I don't have anything to go back to in Arizona."

Finally taking a seat, Barker's face suddenly became pale and weary. "I saw my best friend get blown to pieces last night. Right before my eyes, I saw his bloody body parts scatter into a million pieces flying up into the black smoke in all directions. You couldn't tell his head from his guts. Sir, have you ever seen anyone get blown up?" He asked this question as his deep blue eyes met the weary, concerned eyes of the sergeant.

He patiently waited for a reply.

"No private, I can't say that I have ever seen anyone get blown up. I guess this is because I have only been on the battlefield on a few occasions. I'm what you would call *a conscientious objector.* Because of my religious beliefs I am opposed to carrying a weapon but since I am a superb typist, the Army has allowed me to perform the majority of my military duties off the battlefield."

Pulling out a cigarette, the young private lit it with the click of his lighter. His facial expression was somewhat perplexed. "Well how about that. I've never met anybody who was…what did you say you were, sir?"

"I am *a conscientious objector.*"

Still displaying expressions of confusion, Barker shook his head and slowly removed himself from the chair. "Sir, I better head back. I've stayed here too long already. Sir, I wish you well and I hope you get back home to your family real soon."

"Thank you Private Barker, best wishes to you as well. I…"

Before McWilliams could complete his sentence, the loud squealing sound of sirens began to echo throughout the camp. He could hear the eerie voices of soldiers frantically screaming, "Incoming missiles, incoming missiles, take cover, take cover!"

BOOM!

BOOM!

Missiles hit the camp. Fire, smoke and the smell of burning human flesh was all Sergeant McWilliams remembered before slipping into unconsciousness.

CHAPTER 2

Fort Collins, Colorado, December 21, 1971

"Sweetheart, where are you?" Hurriedly scrambling from room to room yelling, Carol McWilliams was anxiously trying to find her husband to share the exciting news she had just received from her mother. It had been two years since she had seen her parents, but in two days she and her husband, along with their three small children, would make the two-hour trip from Fort Collins to Colorado Springs for the holidays.

Standing on the back porch of their quaint little two-bedroom house was where Carol found her husband. For a brief moment she stood admiring her handsome husband. Richard was tall in stature standing six four and roughly two hundred pounds. Clean cut with smooth brown skin and hazel eyes that enhanced his good looks. Yes Carol considered herself to be one lucky woman.

Carol noticed Richard staring into the crisp cold blue skies, and he appeared to be dazed and perplexed in his thoughts. "That young man in Vietnam had eyes just as blue as the sky you see up there." Pointing his finger towards the clouds, Carol noticed a slight tremble in her husband's hand. She was genuinely concerned about the behavior of her beloved husband.

Since his return from Vietnam almost three year ago, Richard appeared to be withdrawn from reality. On several occasions, he had spoken about a young man that he met in Vietnam. Quite often, he would wake up in the middle of the night, sweating and screaming out the name of someone named, Private Barker. Whenever Carol confronted her husband about his nightmares, he would freeze up saying, "There is no need to bring up the past because it would only open up old wounds."

"Sweetheart, are you okay?"

Now looking in the direction of his wife, Richard's attention suddenly was focused solely on her. "Baby, I'm sorry, will you please forgive me? You know how sometimes I go over the edge a little…from time to time. Since returning home things have been a little difficult for me. It's been hard trying to adjust but just have patience with me, okay? I promise you soon things will get back to normal. Now, what were you trying to tell me?"

Speaking quickly, Carol began her conversation. "Mom called and said that my brother Raymond and my sister Shelia are coming down for the holiday also! Richard, I am so excited, it has been two years since I have seen my brother and my sister, and it is going to be so awesome! Baby, I am so happy! God watched over you and brought you home to me and the children and now I am going back home to see my family! It's going to be the best Christmas ever!"

Staring into the beautiful face of his wife, Richard had to agree that God's mercy and grace had indeed prevailed over him while in Vietnam. He knew that it was a possibility that he, too, could have been among the casualties when the missiles destroyed his camp. Unlike young Private Barker, God had truly spared his life so he could return to the States to be with his wife and children. Yes, this holiday he had so much to be thankful for. Tenderly embracing his wife, Sergeant McWilliams took a moment to bask in his blessings.

Richard was so grateful for his wife. He had met her five years ago at a basketball game his freshman year of college. The first time Richard laid eyes on Carol it was love at first sight. Carol was petite and about five two in height. She had long flowing dark brown hair and beautiful sparking brown eyes. And her warm, friendly smile captivated Richard's heart. On this particular night, his super star attributes had shined superbly. His twenty-point accomplishment on the court had secured his team, the Panthers, a winning championship. It made him the man of the hour.

When the game was over, instead of going out to celebrate with his teammates, Richard decided to return to his dorm to study for a math exam. An unexpected knock at his door led him into a life-changing destiny. When he opened the door, he was very surprised to see Carol standing there with a sweet smile lingering on her face. Unaware that she was interested in him, Richard appeared to be in utter shock. However, when their eyes met, words were not needed to explain the passion they felt for each other. After welcoming her into his dorm room, their bodies were locked in a passionate embrace all night long. After that special night, it was obvious that they were meant to spend a lifetime together and he eagerly asked her parents for her hand in marriage.

Now, almost 5 years later, their love had survived the devastating, drama of Vietnam and he felt truly blessed to be able to hold in his arms the one thing that he knew expressed the unconditional love of God, and that was his wife.

In a soft quiet whisper, he thanked God for sparing his life and the blessed opportunity to return home to share Christmas with his beautiful family.

Yes, this was going to be a memorable Christmas.

CHAPTER 3

Fort Collins, Colorado, December 23

It was a cold icy morning and although the threat of more ice was in the forecast, Richard and his family excitably prepared to travel to Colorado Springs. The weather conditions did not dampen the spirits or provoke any concerns from Richard. He grew up in Ohio and driving in haphazard conditions such as ice and snow was normal for him. A few days after planning his trip to Colorado Springs, Richard's car was sent to the shop for repairs and unfortunately, it would not be ready until after the holidays. But he was grateful that his brother Marvin had loaned him his Volkswagen to make the trip to Carol's parents for the holidays.

Excitably, Richard placed two small suitcases on the floor of the Volkswagen and rushed inside the house to assist Carol with the children.

Glancing at his watch, he realized that if they planned to arrive in Colorado Springs before nightfall, he had less than an hour to load up the car and his family and head for interstate 287.

Hurriedly rushing into the house, Richard saw his four year old daughter Lesley sitting on the floor sucking her thumb. The sweet innocent action of his beautiful little girl almost brought tears to his eyes and he was overwhelmed as compassion pierced his heart. Gently he picked his daughter up from the floor and cradled her in his loving masculine arms. "How's daddy's little girl? Are you ready to go see grandma and grandpa? Where is mommy? Have you seen mommy?"

"I'm right here!"

Richard turned around and saw Carol rushing from the kitchen carrying baby Richard in one arm while juggling the diaper bag and a brown paper bag overflowing with jars of baby food and snacks in the other arm.

"Baby, let me help you!" Richard shouted in concern after her.

"No thanks. I got this. You take Lesley and Selena to the car, and I'll bring the baby and the rest of these things."

"Okay Sergeant Carol, your orders are my command!" Richard playfully replied.

Following his wife's request, Richard immediately grabbed the hands of his daughters, placed them in the car, and buckled them securely into their seat belts. Smiling and glancing down at his beautiful little girls he reflected on how joyful he had been with the birth of each of his daughters. "God, so much time has passed," he whispered to himself. "God, I thank you for sparing my life and bringing me safely back home to my family."

"Baby, I think we're ready to leave now." Carol excitedly spoke as she placed baby Richard Jr. in his car seat.

"Okay, let me check the house one more time to make sure we didn't forget anything." Richard immediately made his way back inside the house for one final check of any forgotten items.

The thought of forgotten items began to linger in Carol's mind and then she remembered that she had left her parent's Christmas presents underneath the Christmas tree. Abruptly, she proceeded to open the car door, but at that moment, she saw Richard bringing the presents to the car. With a sweet gesture, Carol rolled down her window and retrieved the presents from her husband. "Thank you sweetheart," she replied in relief.

Getting into the car, Richard took his wife's small soft hand and lovingly caressed her face drawing her nearer to him. Their lips met and he passionately kissed her warm soft lips. Overwhelmed with emotions, Richard closed his eyes and breathed deeply.

"Carol I love you so much and I am so blessed and I want to thank you for giving me a chance and standing by my side all these years. Baby when we return from our trip, I promise you're going to see a changed man."

Carol smiled and love appeared in her eyes. What her husband did not know was the fact that she was the one who felt extremely blessed that God had chosen her to be his wife.

From the moment she laid eyes on Richard, she knew that he was the only man that she wanted to spend the rest of her life with and grow old together. As she stared into his handsome face, she could feel tears of joy uncontrollably overflowing from her eyes. Immediately Richard gently kissed her tears and apologized for his actions.

"Baby, never apologize when it comes to love," she sweetly sighed.

"True. Well, let's get going I want to try to make it to your parents' before night fall."

"It's early yet and we have lots of time. Besides, I don't want you speeding on this ice in this little car. I don't want us to end up in a ditch." Carol playfully stated.

"Baby don't worry." Richard gently patted his wife's hand and glanced in the back seat of the car where his three precious children were sound asleep.

"I promise I will drive extremely carefully, because I realize that I am carrying precious cargo."

Gently grasping hold of her husband's hands, Carol McWilliams began whispering a prayer for the safe travel of her and her beautiful family. "Dear Lord…"

CHAPTER 4

With less than forty-five minutes left before arriving in Colorado Springs, Richard was grateful that his children and his wife had peacefully slept through some rough icy spots he had to navigate his little yellow Volkswagen over. Still engrossed in his driving, Richard did not hear Carol's request for him to pull over at the next gas station so that she and the girls could use the bathroom. It was not until he had passed the gas station that he finally understood her request.

"Richard? You passed the gas station," Carol quickly stated.

"What? Sweetheart, we do not need gas!"

Richard blatantly replied.

"Baby, we have been driving for two hours and the girls and I really have to go. Besides, you need to stop and stretch those long legs of yours." She gently placed her hand on Richard's knee. Carol's sweet gesture brought a smile to Richard's face, and he agreed to stop at the next gas station.

At that moment, the baby began to cry and Carol unbuckled her seat belt and reached in the back seat for the baby. "Now, now sweet heart, I know you're hungry aren't you?" Her sweet gentle voice seemed to soothe the crying infant and after placing her breast into the baby's mouth, her assumption that the baby was hungry proved true.

"Wow, the way he's going at it on your breast, you would think he was starving!" Richard playfully teased.

"Oh be quiet, you're just jealous that it's the baby Richard and not you!" Carol laughed even though she was embarrassed.

With eyes sparkling with desire Richard glanced over at Carol. "Are you flirting with me Mrs. McWilliams?"

Carol's face appeared somewhat flushed and awkwardness drenched her eyes. "Baby I'm sorry, that did sound a little naughty didn't it? I am so embarrassed."

"Please don't be, I love it when you talk naughty to me, it turns me on."

Looking into Richard's handsome happy face, Carol suggested that they change the topic of discussion so they would not miss the next exit to the gas station.

"Oh look," Richard joyfully shouted, "the sign says there's a station less than two miles ahead."

"Great, let me fasten the baby back into his car seat," Carol replied.

Driving in front of Richard was a beat up, old black Ford truck that was moving so slow, you would think that the driver was asleep at the wheel.

"Now you see people like this person should just pull over to the side of the road and let other drivers pass by."

"It's going to be okay sweetheart. Just take your time and perhaps he'll notice us behind him and he'll pull over." Carol let out an uneasy sigh and weariness was heard in her voice.

Extremely irritated with the slow pace of the driver ahead, Richard made the decision to pass the truck. "I've had enough of this bastard. I know he sees me because he keeps looking in his rear view mirror! If I don't pass him I will miss the exit to the gas station!"

"No Richard!" Carol exclaimed, her voice echoing off into silence. It was too late. Richard had already made the hasty decision to pass the slow moving truck. Suddenly, the small Volkswagen began spinning out of control on the slippery, icy highway.

As Richard struggled to gain control of his car, his vision became impaired from the reflection of bright headlights from an eighteen wheeler coming in his direction. Attempting to avoid the head on collision from the eighteen wheeler, Richard turned his steering wheel and tried to run into a ditch. Unfortunately, his efforts were unsuccessful and with a powerful blow, the eighteen wheeler plowed head on into Richard's car. Rolling over several times, the Volkswagen continued falling downward into a deep dark embankment.

When the car finally came to a squeaking halt, Richard forced himself to look at Carol. Richard noticed blood profusely covering her face. Hysterically screaming Carol's name eagerly and in a panic, Richard gently touched Carol's wrist, praying for a pulse. The one he found was extremely faint.

Richard turned his attention to his children. However, when he turned and glanced into the back seat of the car, he was surprised to find the children were not there. At this moment Richard almost lost his mind. "Oh God! Where are my children?" he screamed with agony. He could see red flashing lights and people running down the embankment. Immediately, he heard the voice of someone shouting, "There are three children over here!"

With an attempt of urgency, Richard got out of the car and tried to make his way up the embankment, but failed to do so because he had injured his ankle. "My wife, my wife is in the car! Please see about my wife!" Richard yelled in agony to a paramedic. With the assistance of a police officer Richard made his way up the embankment and there laid his three children. To his amazement, his two little girls were crying, but appeared to be okay. His son however, appeared to be either unconscious or perhaps dead. Immediately Richard proceeded in the direction of his children. Lifting up his daughters then slowly he kneeled over his son.

A paramedic assisted Richard with his daughters, and informed him that his son has sustained severe head injuries and it was imperative that his son be rushed to a hospital. The paramedic also suggested that Richard's daughters be admitted to a hospital as well. Gazing at his children, suddenly Richard was consumed with unbearable agony and began shaking and crying uncontrollably.

When Richard saw the police officers and the paramedics bringing Carol's lifeless body up from the embankment he rushed over to her side. "Carol! Baby can you hear me?" There was no sign of life from his wife's limp body yet Richard did overhear a paramedic say there was a faint pulse. Richard was clinging onto any type of hope that perhaps Carol would survive. Clinging onto Carol's lifeless body Richard could no longer endure the anguish of this horrific circumstance. From the bottomless pits of his soul, Richard screamed a wailing cry that sent chills down the spines of every by stander. "Oh God! Why did you allow this to happen? Why?

CHAPTER 5

Blytheville, Arkansas, December 23

"Mama! Come quickly, something is wrong with Rachel."

"Eloisa Tatum, what are you shouting about?" Coral Tatum wiped her hands on her apron and made her way into the tiny bedroom of her two daughters. Rachel, her fourteen year old daughter, had come home that afternoon from school with a fever. She had taken a nap, but was now awake.

As she drew near, Coral Tatum could see an odd expression on the face of her daughter. Gently touching her forehead, Coral noticed that Rachel still had a slight fever. "Rachel, baby how do you feel?" she inquired with concern.

Anguish and fear appeared on the face of Rachel Tatum. Her entire body trembled from some sort of unknown terror.

"Sweetheart, please, tell me what's wrong!" Coral Tatum began to express immense concern for her daughter's actions.

Struggling to find words to express what was bothering her, Rachel buried her face into the chest of her mother and tried to find the words to explain the tormented agony which had her so consumed with fear.

"Mommy, I had this bad dream about a man and his family. They were in a really bad car accident!"

Hysterically, Rachel continued, revealing the terrible nightmare that had shaken and mortified her.

"She died mommy, the lady in my dream died! She had three little children and they were in the accident too! It was terrible mommy!" Telling the dream made Rachel even more hysterical and her mother was having difficulty calming her down.

Coral reassured her daughter that she had a nightmare. However, unbeknown to her, in actuality, what her daughter had dreamed had in fact occurred miles away from the small town of Blytheville, Arkansas. Yes, Rachel Tatum's nightmare was a divine revelation of the disastrous results of a decision made by a man who would one day cross her path many years in the future.

CHAPTER 6

Limon Colorado Memorial Hospital

Chaotic turmoil could best describe the events that were taking place inside Limon Colorado Memorial Hospital after Sergeant Richard McWilliams's family was admitted to the trauma ward. It was the nearest hospital to the site of the tragic accident. Richard had notified Carol's family and they had arrived at the hospital before the ambulances that carried Carol and her three small children.

In the hospital waiting room, Richard along with Renee and Harold, (carol's parents) her brother Raymond and her sister Shelia were wearily waiting to hear the prognosis of Carol and the children. It was an unbelievable fate, but Richard's only injury sustained from the accident was a sprained ankle. As the doctor slowly approached the family, Carol's mother observed the sorrowful expression on the doctor's face and she became weak in her knees. Falling to her knees, she began wailing uncontrollably from the bottomless pits of her soul. Carol's mother knew in her heart that her daughter had not survived the accident.

Consolation and comfort was not an option for Carol's mother as she hysterically screamed out her daughter's name. Her heart wrenching screams echoed throughout the hospital as her heart ached with the sorrowful despair of the loss of her youngest daughter.

"Dr. Sanders, is my wife okay? How are my children?" A heart-wrenching plea concerning his family was heard in Richard's voice.

Although Doctor Sander's experience of handling trauma cases had spanned over three decades, he would, at times, encounter heart-wrenching cases such as this one that would rip his heart apart. "Richard, I am so sorry…but your wife did not make it. Because of the impact of the accident, her entire skeletal frame was shattered. There was no way we could have saved her. I am so sorry."

Forcing to make his voice heard among the hysterical chaotic scene, Carol's father immediately inquired about the children. "How are my grandchildren?" he worriedly yelled.

"We are still working on the children and it appears that the girls will make a complete recovery but, unfortunately, your grandson has a severe head concussion and only time will give a better prognosis of his condition."

A nurse informing him that he was needed in surgery interrupted the conversation between Dr. Sanders and Carol's father.

Now alone, faced with the dreadful reality of the loss of Carol, the family members embraced each other, sharing both grief and pain of what would be the most unforgettable hardships they had ever encountered. Among tears of sorrow the utterance of prayers for the miraculous recovery of the children could be heard.

"Oh God! Please do not take the children too! Please, God have mercy on my babies."

Richard's sorrowful cry was one that sent chills down the spines of every listening ear. Overcome with sadness, it appeared that he was going to faint. Suddenly he fell to his knees onto the floor, weeping and crying hysterically. Richard was sedated and was admitted into the hospital on that dark, dreary night. Yes, Richard McWilliams life had been turned upside down and he had lost his most precious gift: his beautiful sweet wife, Carol.

CHAPTER 7

Colorado Springs, Colorado, December 27

On a cold dreary December morning, immediate family members and a few childhood friends privately attended the funeral of Carol McWilliams.

After the funeral, standing alone silently at the gravesite, Richard feverishly screamed out, "Lord why have you done this to me? Why did you take the only person I cherished and loved? Why God have you forsaken me?"

The unbearable grief that had consumed Richard McWilliams could not be consoled with words of comfort from concerned friends and family members. The anguish of Carol's death had immersed his entire being. He repeatedly kept falling to his knees at the gravesite, wailing with painstaking sighs of deep inner remorse and grief. After more than thirty minutes of his mourning, Harold, Carol's father, along with her brother, Marvin, carried Richard from the gravesite so he would not endure the unbearable act of witnessing Carol's body lowered into the deep dark grave.

Unbeknown to Richard, God was about to give him a lesson on who was really in control of his life. Richard did not understand that although his heart was broken from the loss of his precious wife, he would have to come to grips with the fact that God was the master of the universe and He does what he wants when He wants too and nothing was going to interfere with the plans that God had for his life.

Yes, Richard was heartbroken and devastated by the death of his precious wife, but the role that she played on this earth was now over and although it was painful, God ended that period of Richard's life because God had other plans for Richard's future.

In the years to come, time would heal the broken heart of Sergeant Richard McWilliams. However, before emerging from his healing process, he would encounter many unusual situations on his journey.

CHAPTER 8

Fort Collins, Colorado, January 30

A month had passed since Carol McWilliams's untimely death. Still devastated and in a state of shock, Richard, four-year-old Lesley and three-year-old Selena had returned home. He was trying to resume his life to the best of his abilities without his beloved wife Carol. Sadly, he had to leave behind his infant son, Richard Jr., due to his severe injuries. Baby Richard had to remain in the hospital in intensive care for at least two more weeks.

He was grateful that his in-laws had agreed to take on the responsibility of caring for baby Richard until he was well enough to come home. The task of taking care of his two healthy daughters had become overwhelming over the past month, and he could only imagine how difficult it would have been taking on the responsibility of taking care of his son.

Deep in his thoughts, Richard did not hear the repeated ringing of the doorbell, so when a forceful knock on his front door grasped his attention, he jumped. "Who's there?" he quickly asked.

"Richard it's me Clara Mason, your neighbor. I just came by to check on you and the girls. Do you need anything?"

Richard thought for a moment, repeating the name of this unknown woman who had shown up at his front door without an invitation. "Clara who?"

Richard asked in a flat tone.

Resuming her quest, Clara Mason once again announced herself. "Richard, its Clara Mason, I live a few houses down the street from you. I am so sorry to bother you, but I was concerned about you and the children and I just wanted to stop by to see if there was anything I could do for you."

Richard knew for certain that he did not know this woman. In fact, he did not know any of the strangers who had shown up at his front door over the past month. He was an introvert, but Carol had a magnetic personality that was appealing to everyone. He knew the reason his neighbors were coming over was because of the love they had for his beloved Carol.

If he had his way, he did not want to be bothered with any of these intruders he just wanted to be left alone in solitude with his daughters. However, presently, this persistent woman, Clara Mason, was still banging on his door. He knew the only way to stop the annoying actions of this determined woman was to open the door.

When Richard opened the door, he saw that Clara had positioned her hand to knock again. Clara Mason was a tall attractive woman, with beautiful flowing, black hair, and a stunning appearance that illuminated class and style. However, to Richard McWilliams, she was just another annoying neighbor that he wanted to disappear.

"Richard, I was going to knock on your door one more time before I decided to walk away." Her remark was followed by a small crooked smile. Clara quickly extended her hand, and received a brief handshake from Richard. Immediately stepping inside the house, Clara began expressing her sympathy over Carol's death. "I was so heartbroken when I heard about Carol. I know you are grieving right now, and I won't take up much of your time, but if there is anything that you need, please don't hesitate to give me a call." She spoke in a quick compelling manner as if she could feel Richard's emotional state.

"Thank you ma'am for coming by, but me and the children are doing just fine," Richard spoke slowly, as he quickly opened the door for Clara to exit.

"Well…okay this is all I wanted to say so I guess I will let you get back to…whatever, you were doing."

"Thank you ma'am." With those last words, Richard closed the door.

CHAPTER 9

The phone was ringing, and upon answering, a smile immediately came over Richard's s weary face when he heard the voice of his mother-in- law Renee. "Hello Renee, how is my son doing?" He anxiously asked.

"Hello, Richard. He is doing much better in fact, the doctor said he could come home tomorrow."

"Thank God! So when will I be able to come down there to pick him up?" There was a slight pause on the phone. "Renee, did you hear my question?" Richard asked with a perplexed tone.

"Yes Richard, I heard your question, but there is something I need to discuss with you. Harold and I have decided that we need to talk about the matter face to face. We will be out to see you and the girls on Saturday, say about 3 pm?"

"Yes that would be fine, but Renee, what's going on?" Concern could be heard in Richard's voice.

"Richard, please know that the baby is fine, but we need to discuss the wellbeing and the future not only of Richard Jr. but the girls as well. Anyway, we will speak more about the matter when we see you. Kiss the girls for me we will see you in a few days."

"Okay. We will see you on Saturday." The conversation with Renee left Richard wondering what was on her mind. With the passing of each day, there was an uneasy disturbance consuming Richard's thoughts.

Finally, Saturday came and promptly at 3 pm, the much anticipated arrival of his in-laws happened. To the best of his ability, Richard had carefully groomed his two daughters, with the hope that their appearance would be satisfactory to his in-laws.

He watched out the window as the black Cadillac of Carol's parents arrived in the driveway. He continued to watch as he saw Renee lift the car seat carrying his son out the car. Immediately his heart leaped with joy. Slowly placing the blinds back into place, he gathered his daughters and waited for his in-laws to knock on the door.

CHAPTER 10

After the second knock, Richard's trembling hand quickly opened the door. "Renee and Harold please come in!"

"Oh my, look at the girls, don't they look beautiful!" Renee screamed with excitement. Immediately Renee pulled the blanket off the baby and handed him to Richard. "Richard, take a look at your handsome son."

Richard was overcome with joy as he cradled his small fragile son in his arms. Tears filled his eyes and his lips began to tremble.

"Now be careful with his head, because of his concussion he will have to wear a support cap on his head for a few months, but other than that, he's going to be fine," Renee spoke words of assurance to Richard.

"Hello girls," Harold lovingly called out as he gently scooped his granddaughters up into his arms.

"Grandpa!" his granddaughters yelled with excitement. "Well what about me? Aren't you two glad to see me too?" Renee playfully asked.

"Grandma I'm happy to see you too," Lesley yelled.

"Me too!" Little Selena yelled.

"My, my, the girls have really grown and Richard you have them looking so nice."

"Thanks Renee, come in and take a seat. Can I offer you and Harold some water, juice or perhaps something to eat? I prepared some sandwiches for you all, or we could go out to dinner if you like. Or, would you like to rest for while?"

"No Richard, we're fine, son. How are you getting along? I know taking care of two little girls is a big job for you."

"No, Harold, it's not so bad. I suppose when I start working, it might get a little hectic but for now, I am doing just fine. I didn't see any luggage did you bring the baby's things?"

"No Richard, that's what Harold and I wanted to speak to you about."

Immediately Richard sat down, staring at his in-laws with an expression of confusion on his face. "Lesley, take your sister and go play in your room. Grandpa and grandma need to talk to daddy for a moment."

"Daddy can we take the baby with us?"

"No Lesley, your brother has to stay with me, but I'll bring him into your room when we have finished talking. Okay?"

"Okay daddy."

After Richard's daughters left the room, Renee immediately began the conversation. "Richard, as you know the baby's injuries were severe and the doctors have suggested that it would best if the baby remain with us in Colorado Springs in order to assure a full recovery.

This way, he could remain under the same doctors who are familiar with his medical history and so forth. Therefore, Harold and I would like custody of Richard Jr. In addition, we think that it would be a good idea if you allow us to keep the girls as well. This way, the children will not be separated and can be raised together."

"Yes son, Renee, and I think it would be in the best interest of the children, and as you know, we are better financially prepared to support the children."

"Stop…Just stop!" Richard spoke with a calm yet angry tone. "I can't believe you two! You come into my home and try to take away the only people I have left in my life that I love? How dare you!"

"Richard, we mean you no harm, but we are only thinking about what is best for the children! Please be reasonable!"

"Reasonable? I can take care of my children!

And you know this is not what Carol would have wanted!"

"Richard please! We would like to settle this matter between us, without getting attorneys involved!"

"Attorneys!" Richard was outraged after Renee mentioned an attorney. "You would actually take me to court to take my children away from me?"

Holding his son, Richard abruptly stood up from the sofa and rushed towards the door. Opening the door, Richard spoke to his in-laws in a harsh tone. "I think it's time you left my house."

"Give me the baby!" With outstretched arms, Renee demanded that Richard hand over her grandson. "Richard we are not leaving here without the baby!"

Richard stood motionless and did not react to Renee's demand.

"Richard, son, please be reasonable. The baby is in no condition to remain here with you. He still needs lots of medical attention and if he remains here, you are putting him in jeopardy of not making a full recovery.

Richard we know you are upset right now, but please just think this thing through. Let us take the baby back with us and after you have cooled down, we can sit down again and discuss what will be best for the children. Renee and I only want what is best for our grandchildren. Renee and I both know in our hearts that our daughter would not have wanted us to be bickering amongst each other.

Please Richard, I'm begging you, let us take the baby back to Colorado Springs."

Staring unresponsively, a dismal expression of defeat came over Richard's face. He knew in his heart that he was not in a position to provide the proper medical care for his son and he did not want to be the reason for his son not making a complete recovery.

After all, if the truth were to be known, he himself was still dealing with the guilt that the accident was his fault. Each day, he was tormented by voices that had convinced him that he had killed his wife and injured his children.

"Richard, did you hear what I said?"

"Yes Harold, I heard you. And you're right."

With those spoken words, Richard walked off in the direction of his daughters' bedroom. Slowly opening the door, his daughters rushed to his side. "Girls, say goodbye to your baby brother, he's leaving now. Your grandparents will bring him back for a visit another time."

Lesley and Selena both kissed their little brother and told him they loved him very much. Afterwards, Richard placed his son into the arms of Renee and without hesitation Harold and Renee took the small infant and walked out the door. Solemnly standing in the doorway, Richard and his two daughters were waving goodbye when suddenly the unwelcomed appearance of his neighbor Clara caught him off guard. This was an inappropriate moment because Clara was the last person that Richard wanted to see.

Ignoring her presence, Richard took the hands of his daughters and proceeded inside the house.

"Richard is everything okay?"

Richard continued his entrance into the house, and did not reply to Clara's question.

"Richard did you hear me?"

"Clara, I'm sorry but I cannot talk to you right now." Swiftly, Richard closed the door in Clara's face.

CHAPTER 11

Six months after the death of Richard's wife, he decided it was time to return to work. Since returning from his duties in Vietnam, Richard had taken a position as an army recruiter on base. In his opinion, the highlight of being a recruiter was going into various schools to speak to students about the advantages of enlisting into the military.

The moment Richard walked into his office he was greeted by his co-workers who expressed words of encouragement and sympathy concerning the loss of his wife.

"Richard we're so glad to have you back in the saddle. Are things going well for you? I mean are you doing okay?"

"Yes sir, Major Reed, I'm hanging in there considering all that has happened over the past few months. But I can say that it's good to be back. I decided it was time to come out of seclusion and get back into the swing of things. And as you know, I have kids to feed and bills to pay."

"Yes, I do understand, and how are the children doing?"

"Major Reed, they're doing okay. They're in the daycare here on the base. I have to admit that I felt sad when I dropped them off this morning. For the past few months, they've been at home with me."

"Richard don't worry they will be just fine, you know my girls are in the base daycare as well. The teachers are awesome and are really attentive to the needs of the children. After all that has happened, the girls need to be in an environment with other children."

"Yes you're right, they will be fine. So, I'm ready to get to work. Major Reed, do you have anything at any of the schools I could check out?"

"As a matter of fact I do. I have two schools in the area you could visit today."

Richard was back in the saddle so to speak. He was excited to be back at work because being at work gave him a sense of focus and belonging. For months, he had sat at home grieving the loss of his wife. However, Richard realized that now he had the responsibility taking care of his children.

Richard knew if he was going to keep his daughters and regain custody of his son, he had to focus on the important matter at hand, which was being a responsible father. This was all he had to live for now: being the best father he could be for his children. No matter what it took, he would go to hell and back to keep his children.

CHAPTER 12

"Richard?"

"Hello Renee, how's my son doing?"

"He's coming along quite well. In fact, Harold and I just returned from the doctor's office and he has been released from the doctor and we were informed that with therapy he should make a full recovery."

"This is great news! So when can I come get my son and bring him home? The girls ask about him every day."

"That's what I am calling you about, Richard. You see, Harold and I have filed a petition to take full custody of Richard Jr. and the girls. We think it would be in the best interest of all the children if they were raised together in a stable environment. If they lived with us they would have access to the best schools and would live in a two parent home.

You, on the other hand, would be a struggling single father trying to raise three small children, on a limited income, living on a military base. So it is in the best interest of the children that…"

"Renee stop it! I don't want to hear any more of your bull shit! I will not give up custody of my children to you and Harold or anyone else. If I have to get an attorney and fight for my rights, I will do so!"

"Richard, be reasonable. You know you are not in a financial position to hire an attorney to fight against Harold and me. And besides, no judge is going to agree to give you custody of my grandchildren not after what you have done!"

"After what I've done? Renee what do you mean after what I have done?"

"You killed my daughter! I blame you for the accident! I know there could have been some way you could have prevented the accident. Harold spoke to the driver of the truck that you were trying to pass and he said there was no way in hell that you should have tried to pass him! You passed him in a curve and there was no way you could have seen the oncoming traffic.

Richard, I will never forgive you there is no way in hell I will allow you to keep my grandchildren. If it takes every penny I have, I will fight you to hell and back before I allow you to get custody of my grandchildren. I am so afraid that you might kill them too! So if you want to fight us, you will get a fight! I will see you in court!"

With those last words, Renee abruptly hung up the phone. Richard stood there for several minutes, emotionally distraught and consumed with shock and pain from the heart wrenching conversation he had just had with his mother in law.

Falling to his knees, Richard cried out in agony with a loud raucous scream, "Oh God please help me! You took my wife please don't take my children too!"

CHAPTER 13

Clara had not seen Richard for several weeks so one afternoon she decided to check on him. She walked onto Richard's porch and with a quick gesture she started knocking on his door. "Hello, Richard are you in there? Is everything alright?"

For the last fifteen minutes or so, Richard had himself a pity party. Now with the sudden interruption from this annoying woman he quickly got up from the floor and tried to pull himself together.

Frantically, Clara continued knocking on Richard's door. "Hello? Richard are you in there?"

Reluctantly, Richard walked over and opened the door. With a slow sorrowful tone, he confronted Clara. "Clara how are you?" He kept his head bowed fearing that Clara would detect the redness of his eyes brought on by his tears.

"Richard, are you okay? I was jogging past your house and I heard this dreadful scream coming from your house! Are the girls okay?"

"Yes, they're still at day care, I was just on my way out to pick them up." Richard turned his back to Clara and reached into his pocket to retrieve his car keys.

"So, if the girls are at day care, then that means it was you who was screaming." Placing her hand on Richard's, Clara began to console him. "Richard, I know over the last year how you have endured the pain of losing Carol. But please know that if you need anything, I am here to help you through this." Clara's voice was sweet and lingered with empathy.

Suddenly Richard was overtaken by a rush of sorrowful, uncontrollable emotions that consumed his entire being. He began shaking and weeping and at that moment, he was not concerned about his macho image. His only concern was to release the agonizing pain that he had held within his heart since the death of Carol.

Gently, Clara placed her small delicate hand on Richard's face and began wiping away his tears. In a sweet concerned voice, Clara whispered, "Richard, please let me help you. Whatever you need me to do… I will do it."

Slowly Richard asked Clara a surprising question.

"Clara, will you marry me?"

A shocked expression came over Clara's face. "Marry you? I don't understand?" Clara was in a quandary.

"My children need a mother. My in-laws are threatening to take my children and I cannot let this happen. The way I see it, if I had a wife, I would have a better chance of retaining full custody of my children. So, if you are really sincere about helping me, then marry me."

Perplexed and dazed, for once in her life, Clara was speechless for a brief moment. "Let me get back with you, okay? I have to think about this sudden proposal." With that statement Clara quickly made her exit out the front door. Bewildered, Richard concluded that he had made a terrible mistake asking Clara to marry him because her reaction to the question had made him feel like a fool. However, the conversation with his mother- in-law had pushed him over the edge, and whatever he had to do, he would do because of his desperation to keep his children. No, Clara did not say yes to his proposal, but she did not say no either.

CHAPTER 14

Three days had passed since Richard made his unexpected marriage proposal to Clara. Her non-responsive reply convinced him that his actions had chased Clara off for good. He felt like an idiot! How could he ever face her again?

In fact, how could he ever face his neighbors? He assumed that Clara had told everyone in the neighborhood about his marriage proposal. He could not change what he did, so whatever gossip was being spoken about him, he would just have to endure. Right now, his main objective was to keep his children.

"Oh well, it is what it is," he murmured in a slow tone. "Let me see what am I'm going to do with myself on my day off. The kids are in day care until six and I don't know what to do." Brushing his finger over a table, Richard murmured, "I could give the house a good cleaning. Yep, that's what I'll do, then if I have some time to spare, I think I'll treat myself to a movie, and afterwards I'll pick the girls up, and take them out for pizza. Yep, that's what I'm going to do."

Two hours went by and Richard had almost completed his cleaning chores when he heard someone knocking at his door. Holding a can of furniture polish and an old dust cloth, Richard quickly opened the door. He was both surprised and embarrassed to see Clara standing there.

"Clara!"

"Hello Richard, may I come in?"

"Sure, excuse the mess. Today is my off day and I was just doing a little cleaning. Would you like to sit down?"

Pacing back and forward, Clara appeared nervous and irritable. "No, I would rather stand. Richard, I came over to discuss your marriage proposal. I'm sorry it's taken me a few days to come over to talk to you, but I had to really think about your proposal. Are you sure this is what you want to do? I mean, it has only been a year since Carol passed away."

"I'm sorry Clara, I would understand if you said no. But I told you the circumstances concerning my request to get married. I need a wife otherwise, I might lose custody of my children."

"Yes, I understand, and I have taken these few days to consider your request. This is why I came over to tell you that I will marry you."

Richard was overjoyed by Clara's answer, and he tenderly hugged her to express his gratitude.

"Richard, what really helped me to make my decision, was after I discussed your proposal with a few of my girlfriends and they all agreed that marrying you to help take care of your children would be the noble thing for me to do. I know you have been through so much and I just want to bring a little happiness into your life."

Moving closer to Richard, Clara continued her conversation. "If you ask me, I'm the one who's hit the jackpot. I am getting a good man and two beautiful little girls. What more can I ask for?" Clara yelled with excitement. "I'm ready to get married today!"

"Clara, I have three children. I also have a son. He is with his grandparents right now, but I want custody of my son too."

"Yes, I forgot you do have a son, he was born a month after I moved here."

"Clara, I have to be honest with you. You know the main reason I asked you to marry me is because I am trying to get custody of my children. Right? I am not in love with you. The way I see it if I had a wife, the judge might consider giving me custody of my three children. Can you understand my predicament?" Richard's gazed at Clara with concern.

Caressing Richard's hands and compassionately gazing into his sorrowful eyes, Clara began to comfort Richard. "Richard, sweetheart, I understand. You don't love me, but I do love you. I have loved you since the first day I saw you. I use to tell my girlfriends, that Carol is one lucky woman. I know I can never replace Carol, but sweetheart, I will try to be a good wife and a good mother to your children." Stretching her hand out to Richard, Clara asked. "Can we shake on it?"

"Sure." Richard replied.

"So, when are we getting married?"

"Well I would like to tell my girls and my family before we start making plans."

"Okay, I'll tell my girlfriends and my family after you speak to everyone. Are we going to have a wedding?"

"Clara, I don't think that would be necessary."

"I understand. Whatever you want, Richard. When you're ready, we'll set a date, and go to the Justice of the Peace. But, could we have a nice little reception afterwards so our family and friends can celebrate our happy day?"

"Sure, Clara make all the plans and let me know how much everything will cost."

"Okay that sounds great! Just let me know when you make your decision. Well, I better be going and let you get back to your house cleaning, or did you need me to help you with anything?"

"No I got this. Once again, I would like to say thank you for accepting my proposal. I will forever be in your debt. I will be a good husband to you Clara."

"Good bye Richard, I'll see you tomorrow, perhaps?"

"Yes, I'll talk to my girls this afternoon and I'll let you know something tomorrow."

When Clara left, Richard felt a small flicker of hope rise within his heart. No, no one could ever replace his beautiful wife, Carol but Clara was a beautiful, good-hearted woman, and he made a promise to himself that with all his might, he would always cherish Clara for the goodness she had shown him.

Richard's private conversation was interrupted by an unexpected knock on his door. "Who could that be?" When Richard opened the door, he was surprised see Clara's glowing face. "Clara what's wrong?"

"Richard nothing's wrong, but I was almost home when I remembered that I forgot to tell you that I loved you. After speaking these sincere words to Richard, Clara waited for a moment expecting a reply from Richard.

Richard's mind wildly wondered not knowing what to say to Clara. "Clara we just had a discussion concerning how I felt about you. Now if this is going to be a problem, maybe we should just call this thing off."

"No, I'm sorry. I guess I'm just expecting too much from you right now. But I know in time you will learn to love me. Don't worry I won't bring up this topic again. So, I'll talk to you later."

For some odd reason Clara continued staring at Richard. Her stare made him extremely uncomfortable and he felt as if a hole was burning into his heart. So without hesitation, Richard yelled, "Yes Clara with time, there is a possibility that I could learn to love you!"

With a sense of satisfaction Clara embraced Richard and whispered into his ear. "Thank you Richard! I am so happy! So, I'll get out of your way, because I know you have things to do and so do I."

Clara planted a wet, juicy kiss on Richard's lips and once again she made her exit. Slowly Richard closed the door and sorrowfully murmured, "God what am I getting myself into?"

CHAPTER 15

Colorado Springs, CO

Six months after Richard and Clara's marriage, the court proceedings for the custody of his children began. Returning to the place where he had buried his wife brought both sadness and grief to his heart. However, Richard had made the decision to visit his beloved Carol's grave site before he left Colorado Springs.

Richard had high expectations that his marriage to Clara would be the solution to him gaining full custody of his children, but unfortunately, the first day of the hearing proved to be a complete disappointment. To his misfortunate, his in-laws had hired one of the most prominent attorneys that money could buy. His name was Roger Hankins and he had a reputation of ripping out the hearts of his defendants.

When Richard took the witness stand, Mr. Hankins crucified him! Richard was questioned about his diagnosis of post-traumatic stress, he was questioned about the different types of medication he was taking, and Mr. Hankins expressed his concern about the long-term effects these medications would have on Richard's mental state of mind.

Mr. Hankins expressed his concerns of how Richard's medication could have possibly caused the accident that killed his wife! In addition, if the knife had not been dug deep enough into Richard's heart, Mr. Hankins ordered Richard to step down from the witness stand, and had a psychologist take the stand to validate that there was a possibility that these assumptions concerning Richard's condition were possibly valid.

The psychologist proceeded to express his concern for the safety of the children if they were in Richard's permanent care.

When Richard's mother in-law Renee took the stand, her performance was so dramatic, to the point that he knew that he did not have a chance in hell of gaining custody of his children. However, the nail that sealed the coffin was when his new wife, Clara, took the witness stand. Mr. Hankins, the attorney for his in-laws, had dug up ten years of incriminating evidence against Clara, which would indisputably disqualify her from being a suitable mother for the children.

Clara had a rap sheet, which included assault with a deadly weapon, fraud, hot check writing, and substance abuse. Her attempts of providing an explanation concerning these charges made her appear even more ridiculous. Frankly, at that moment, her explanation did not matter because the fact that she had a criminal record of any sort was the most damaging fact of all.

Stepping down from the witness stand, Clara immediately rushed over to Richard's side. With a heartfelt determination, she proceeded to explain the reason for the charges. "Richard I am so sorry, I had no idea that the attorney was going to dig up my past!"

"Clara, is it true?"

"Some of it is true, but Richard you have to understand, we're talking about the late 60's and the early 70's. Back then I was a radical, pot smoking, kid. Surely you can relate to what I'm saying!"

"Clara, please stop talking!" Richard tried to whisper in a low tone to Clara, but anger would not allow him to do so. "We'll discuss this when we leave the courtroom, what's done is done."

The judge informed everyone that he would make his decision the next day concerning the case, so court was adjourned until 9am the following day.

Once outside the courtroom, Richard roughly grabbed Clara by the arm and began walking out of the building at an exceptionally fast pace. When they got outside, he let out the fury he was holding inside his heart. "Do you know what you just did?" Richard yelled. His spit began flying onto Clara's drained, fearful face. "You have just screwed up my chances of getting my children! There is no way in hell the judge is going to rule in my favor now after finding out that my wife is a damn criminal!"

Frantically sobbing, Clara managed to whisper in a trembling voice, "Richard I am so sorry, please forgive me! Just tell me what you want me to do, so I can fix this and I will do it!"

"I don't think there's anything that can be done. We have to wait until tomorrow to see what the judge says and we'll go from there." Lovingly, Richard embraced Clara and apologized for his angry behavior. "Clara, I am sorry, I didn't mean to yell at you. I'm just so frustrated that you didn't reveal all this baggage from your past."

"Richard..."

Gently placing his finger to Clara's trembling lips, Richard assured her that there was no need to explain her past to him, because whatever skeletons revealed in the courtroom that day would remain locked away.

Richard had concluded that if it were in the cards, then tomorrow the verdict would be in his favor.

CHAPTER 16

The following day at 9am Richard returned to court alone. Clara had agreed to remain at the hotel with the girls. Something she should have considered doing the day before. Perhaps the blunder that she made in court could have been avoided.

Slowly sitting next to his attorney, Richard glanced and saw the approach of his in-laws. "Richard," Harold spoke in a solemn slow tone. "Son, whatever happens here today, please know that we are only thinking about what is best for the children. We have no animosity towards you, Richard."

"Harold, just stop! I don't want to talk to you or Renee right now!"

"Richard, please..." Renee's conversation did not begin because the bailiff started to call the court into session.

"All rise, The Superior Court of the State of Colorado, the Honorable Judge Ross Jones presiding, court is now in session." After the judge entered the court room, the court proceedings began.

Slowly with a southern tone, the judge began his decision concerning the case. "Ladies and gentlemen, I must confess that I have found myself in a very perplexing situation concerning this case. The events that this case is based upon are in my opinion, both heartbreaking and complicated.

Either way, the decision that I make here today, will bring heartache and pain to the other parties. However, I strongly believe my decision is in the best interest of the children. Sergeant McWilliams, Mr., and Mrs. Foster, would you please stand? Mr. and Mrs. Foster it is my decision that the daughters of Sergeant McWilliams should remain with their father. I have thoroughly done my research concerning the creditably of Sergeant McWilliams, by speaking to his commanding officer, the girls daycare center, and numerous other individual who have nothing but the highest respect for the Sergeant. And I do not foresee any reason why his daughters should not remain in his custody."

Gloom and disappointment could be seen on the faces of Harold and Renee Foster. However, joy and relief suddenly was reflected on the face of Richard McWilliams.

"Regarding my decision of the baby, Richard Jr., I have consulted with the doctors with whom the child has been treated since the disastrous incident that took place a year ago. The court has decided that it would be in the best interest of the child if he remained in the care of his grandparents, Mr. and Mrs. Foster. Because of the child's medical condition, and because of the familiarity that his grandparents have concerning his medical conditions, it would be best if the child remained with them.

At a later date, and if the medical condition of the child improves as time goes on, Sergeant McWilliams, you will have another opportunity to petition for custody of your son. However, for now, I will grant you visitation rights to see your son. You will have the opportunity to see him twice each month. I hope you and Mr. and Mrs. Foster will be able to work together to decide these dates. I am also giving the Fosters visitation rights to see their granddaughters twice each month.

Sergeant McWilliams may I suggest when you visit your son this would be the perfect opportunity to bring your daughters with you and this would give their grandparents the opportunity to see them as well.

Now you two attorneys get together with your clients and work things out. Are there any other requests to be made at this time?"

"Your honor, my clients, the Fosters, would like to request two weeks custody of their granddaughters in the summer and perhaps some holidays."

"Thank you, Attorney Hankins. Sergeant McWilliams do you and your attorney have a problem honoring this request?"

"No your honor, I do not have a problem allowing my daughters to spend this time with their grandparents."

"Well, if there is nothing else, I will adjourn the court. I would like to meet with both attorneys in my chambers, so we can close out this file. Court is now adjourned."

Unexpectedly, Richard's in-laws approached him as he made his way out the courtroom. "Richard, please know that taking you to court was not meant to indicate that you were not capable of caring for our grandchildren. We were only trying to do what was best for the children."

"Harold, Renee, I understand and there are no hard feelings towards either of you. I know you love your grandchildren. However, I love them as well and there is nothing I wouldn't do for my children. I owe this to Carol. Moving forward, let's try to work together so we can take care of her beautiful babies. Agreed?"

"Yes Richard, and if there is anything that the girls need, please don't hesitate to contact Renee and I. Okay?"

"Harold thank you. I will talk to you and Renee soon, but right now, I have to make one stop before I go to the hotel to tell Clara and the girls the good news!"

With those last words, Richard hurriedly made his way out of the courtroom. He caught a cab and went directly to the cemetery where Carol was buried. Standing by her grave tears began to fill his eyes as he whispered a pray to his beloved Carol. "Carol my love, thank you. I could feel your presence today when I was fighting for our children. I miss you so much my love. Until we meet again."

CHAPTER 17

Blytheville, Arkansas

"Rachel are you sure this is what you want to do?"
"Mom please!" Rachel spoke with frustration. You said I could not join the Navy, you said I could not go to Washington. So yes, I am going to Dallas!"

"Sweet heart, I just want you to be happy with your decision."

"Mom I gotta get out of this town! I am so sick and tired of being here! If I don't get out of here, I'm going to lose my mind! I'm going to Dallas and enroll at the Junior college for the fall, and if I don't like it there, I promise I'll come back home and enroll at the little college up town."

"Okay. That sounds fair enough. Sweetheart, please go with my blessings and I want you to be a good girl and do what your cousin Sandra tells you to do. Respect her house just as you have respected our house. Don't be hanging out late at night, and when you get settled, find yourself a little job so you will be able to support yourself."

"Coral, don't worry, I will take good care of your little girl just like she was my own daughter."

"Sandra, I know you will take care of Rachel. It's just that she has never been away from home and…"

Standing in the distance, Rachel's father, Carl Tatum, had been observing the conversation between his daughter, his wife Coral, and Cousin Sandra. Now he felt that it was time to end this ongoing conversation. "Ladies, stop fretting yourselves over Rachel. She will be just fine. She is not a baby she is a beautiful, intelligent seventeen-year-old young woman, and it is time she got out in the world and come into her own. I left home when I was thirteen years old. Yes, I made many mistakes, but I counted them up as learning experiences. And whatever mistakes Rachel makes, they will be her leaning experiences as well. Therefore, baby, I give you my blessings as you go on your journey. However, remember, whatever obstacles you encounter, your mother and I will always be here for you. Okay?"

"Thank you Daddy, I love you."

"We love you too sweetheart. Now I think you and your cousin Sandra should be getting on the road while there is still day light."

"You're right Carl, we should head out. I will call you guys when we make it into Dallas."

As Rachel and Cousin Sandra drove off, Rachel's face beamed with excitement. She was young, eager, and trilled to have the opportunity to leave Arkansas. Yes, Rachel had big dreams for her life and was anticipating a bright future in Dallas. She vowed to herself that she would make her parents proud.

CHAPTER 18

Dallas, TX Six Months Later

"Rachel, what is wrong with you? You've been sleeping a lot and did I hear you vomiting in the bathroom this morning around 3am?" Cousin Sandra demanded a reply as she confronted Rachel.

"I'm 3 months pregnant," Rachel replied with remorse and regret.

"What?" Sandra screamed with a blood-chilling scream. "No, you can't be pregnant! Your parents are going to hate me for allowing this to happen! Don't you understand, I promised them that I would take care of you! Now what will they think?"

Perplexed, Rachel responded to Sandra's reply.

"This is not your fault. I did this. This was my stupid mistake. When I speak to my parents, I'll make it perfectly clear that you did your part of taking care of me."

"Rachel how did this happen? I mean, you're going to school full time and working a part time job, when did you have time to have sex! And with who?"

"It happened after school a few months ago. I have been dating this person named David Ryan. He is a math tutor at the college. We had sex once, but it was unprotected sex. I know it was stupid of me to have unprotected sex, but it just happened." Rachel lowered her head, because she became overtaken with guilt and shame.

"For God sakes child, you could have caught AIDS, or a sexual transmitted disease having unprotected sex! What were you thinking? Have you been tested for any of these diseases?" Sandra asked with a sound of hysteria in her voice.

"Yes Cousin Sandra, when I had my pregnancy test done, all these test were performed. They were all negative."

"Thank God, at least we don't have to worry about you dying from a disease. Rachel, don't beat yourself up. What is done is done. You can't cry over spilled milk. Now you have two choices. Either you're going to keep the baby or you're going to have an abortion." Reaching for Rachel's small quivering hands, Sandra assured Rachel that whatever she decided, she would be there to support her. "If you decide to have the baby, you can still continue living here with me. I see no reason why anything should change. I don't know what you and the father have discussed concerning this matter, but I'm just letting you know that you still have a home here with me."

With those words of assurance from her cousin, a small smile lingered on Rachel's tear stained face. As she began to speak, her words were with disbelief that her cousin would still consider allowing her to live in her house. "I'm so sorry that I disappointed you."

Without speaking a word, Sandra drew Rachel's fragile trembling body to hers. Wrapping her arms around Rachel, she continued to console her struggling emotions. "There, there baby, let it all out. Cry until you can't cry anymore. It is going to be okay. Trust me you're not the first or the last woman to become an unwed mother. Hell, it happened to me when I was only sixteen. So, I know exactly the torment that you're going through."

"Thanks cousin Sandra but, my biggest fear is telling my parents! I know they're going to be so disappointed in me. I promised them that I would come to Dallas and enroll in school and not lay up with some person that I barely know and get pregnant! I've failed them! My parents had great expectations for my life."

"Rachel, life goes on my dear. If you decide to have the baby afterwards you can continue your education. I did it. After I had my daughter Sarah, I went back to school and got my Bachelor's degree and then three years later I went back to school and earned my Masters. So I am living proof that it can be done."

For a brief moment, Rachel said nothing. It appeared that a rush of thoughts raced through her mind. Then suddenly she spoke with a stern tone. "You're right. I am eighteen, I am an adult. I'll get a job and take care of my baby, and once I am established financially, I'll go back to school and get my degree. My parents will have to understand my position. But if they don't, then there's nothing I can do about how they feel."

Expressing support, Sandra yelled, "That's my girl! Everything will work out just fine. Now let's not prolong the news." Reaching for the phone, Sandra began dialing Rachel's parents.

"We're telling them the news now?" Rachel spoke with hesitation and fear.

"Yes, there is no reason to put this off any longer. I'm the type of person who believes that the sooner you put the hard things behind you your mind will be free and clear to walk into your future. So yes, we're calling them right now."

The call was made to Rachel's parents. Yes, her parents were disappointed that she was pregnant. However, to her surprise, they informed her that she could depend on them for support.

With a sigh of release, Rachel's fears subsided. Her mind was free from anxiety and she started to focus on her future. It still was unclear if the father of her baby would be involved in her and the baby's life. However, it didn't matter because she had always been an independent individual and now that she was going to be responsible for the life growing inside of her it would only make her diligently strive toward achieving her goals. "Let the games begin," she quietly whispered to herself.

CHAPTER 19

Fort Collins, CO

Utter turmoil could best describe the crumbling state of Richard and Clara's marriage. Over the past several years, Clara had gotten involved in a strange religious cult that was causing conflict and tension within the marriage. The display of her compelling manner was confirmation that eventually, disastrous results would surely occur.

Clara's late nights of attending undisclosed meetings and frequent trips out of town had begun to send Richard into a raged frenzy. "Enough is enough, tonight when she gets home I'm going to put an end to this crap." Richard was determined to put a stop to Clara's involvement in her new found religion.

After putting the girls to bed, Richard went into the living room, turned off the lights and sat on the couch. Staring at the door, and constantly glaring at his watch, the hours slowly ticked by. "Eight thirty pm, where could this woman be?" He was filled with anger and concern because Clara had been gone since seven that morning and she had not called to inform Richard of her whereabouts.

Ten pm. Richard was pacing the floor with a slow stride of frustration. Still Clara was a no show.

Then at 10:30, Richard heard the turning of the key in the front door. Richard watched as Clara quietly opened the front door. Entering very quietly she made her entrance. Sitting quietly in the shadows of darkness, Richard spoke words that took Clara completely by surprise. "Clara, where have you been?"

Shocked by Richard's unexpected actions, Clara gasped with a loud scream. "Richard! Why are you sitting here in the dark? You frightened me!"

"I'm sitting here because all day, I've been waiting on you to come home! Now answer my question, where have you been?"

"Richard it has been a long day, so I am going to take a shower and I'm going to bed. We will talk about this in the morning, okay?"

"No! It is not okay Clara. This foolishness has got to stop, do you understand? I want you to quit this cult or whatever this crazy religion you have gotten yourself involved in so we can start acting like a family again! Even the girls have started noticing that you're not at home anymore. Clara if you have gotten yourself into something that you can't handle, please talk to me and maybe I can help you in some way. But this going out of town and attending these long secret meetings has to stop!"

At that moment, Clara walked up to Richard and stared him directly in the face. Her piercing black eyes gave a cold and wicked glare and her face was so close to Richard's, until he could feel her hot saliva spattering onto his face when she began to speak. "You will not tell me what to do!

I will do whatever, I want, when I want to! Richard, you don't care about me! We both know the only reason you married me in the first place was to have a mama for your kids! So, now you have them are you happy Richard? Can I have my freedom now?"

Now it was Richard's chance to be shocked and appalled by Clara's sudden confession. "Quiet! Keep your voice down before you wake the girls. Clara are you saying that you want a divorce? Is this why all of sudden you started taking trips out of town and started staying away from home all the time? Just tell me the truth. Are you having an affair?" Richard inquired as he quickly reached for Clara's hand.

"No Richard, I'm not having an affair! But Rashad has instructed me to take a sabbatical from my family to prepare for my induction into his church."

"Wait, back up! First of all, who in the hell is Rashad? And what induction into what church are you talking about?" At this point, Richard was almost over the edge.

"Rashad is my spiritual leader and you know what Richard, he said you would act just like you're acting now! He warned me that you wouldn't understand and that you would be against my beliefs!"

"You see what I mean? I knew you had gotten yourself mixed up in some sort of cult. The first thing in the morning, you're taking me to meet this Rashad, or whatever his name is, and I'm going to make him release you from this mess! Do you understand?"

"No! I am not taking you anywhere because I am not leaving the church! As I said, you can't tell me what to do anymore! So let go of my arm! I will sleep on the sofa tonight and tomorrow I'll pack my things and get the hell out of your house!" At that moment, Clara stormed out of the room.

Richard was standing there dumfounded, with disbelief and hurt lingering on his face. After his conversation with Clara, it appeared that all hope was lost concerning his marriage. His energy was drained from the exhausting conversation with his wife. Slowly he made his way into the bedroom and collapsed into the bed and fell sound to sleep.

About 3am Richard was awakened by a blood chilling scream from his daughter, Lesley. "Daddy wake up!" When Richard opened his eyes, he was shocked to see Clara standing over him with a cross and a hammer in her hands.

Clara's appearance was unrecognizable. She had a chilling blank stare that covered her face and her piercing black eyes darted from side to side with a fast bizarre motion. When Richard called out her name, Clara did not respond and she appeared to be in a delusional trance.

Forcefully, Richard wrestled Clara to the floor, removing the items from her hands. "Clara what in hell are you doing?" Fear mingled with anger could be heard in Richard's trembling voice.

"What's wrong daddy?" Consumed with fear and confusion, Richard's daughter was screaming and crying because she didn't understand what was happening and neither did Richard. "Lesley please go back to bed sweetheart before you wake up your sister, daddy will be fine." Richard's attempt was to comfort his daughter, but in actuality he was emotionally gripped with panic from Clara's actions.

"Daddy are you sure you're okay? Should I call the police?" Lesley asked with momentous concern.

"No sweetheart, don't call the police. Daddy can handle this, I promise you, I will be fine. Now please go back to the bedroom and Lesley, lock the door to your bedroom. Daddy will come to your room in a few minutes. Okay?

"Okay daddy." Slowly with hesitation, Lesley went back to her room. "Clara! What in hell is going on with you? Were you trying to kill me? Richard asked with a tone of overwhelming anger.

"Richard get the hell off me!" Clara angrily screamed.

"Not until you tell me what you were trying to do! You had a cross and a hammer standing over my bed, and if Lesley hadn't come into the room, you probably would have killed me in my sleep! So did this Rashad tell you to kill me? Was I supposed to be some sort of sacrifice?"

Coldly, Clara spoke. "Yes! In order for me to be accepted into the church, Rashad instructed me to sacrifice you and tomorrow morning I was supposed to bring pictures of the sacrifice as evidence that I carried out his instructions." Clara's words were canny, expressing shrewdness toward Richard.

Richard was astonished by Clara's statement and for a brief moment he laid there staring into the face of a woman whose mind apparently had been taken over by the devil. "I'm going to let you up, and when I do, I want you to get the hell out of my house and I don't ever want to see you again. Don't come near me or my children!

Don't contact them or me ever again. Because if you do Clara, I will kill you! Do you understand?"

"Yes, I understand. But what about my clothes and..."

"As I said, when I let you up, walk out that door and I don't ever want to see you again. You will walk out of here with your life. After the crap you pulled here tonight you should consider yourself one lucky woman that you are still alive.

Leave your keys on the desk on your way out. Do you understand, Clara?" Richard spoke with a firmness to make his demands clear to Clara.

Without remorse, Clara replied to Richard. "Yes Richard I understand." Clara's words were callous and harsh.

Slowly and cautiously, Richard removed his stiff six four frame off Clara's petite body. He attentively watched as she reached into her purse and laid the keys to the house on the small black desk by the door entrance. Speechless and with quickness, she ran out the door, slamming it as she made her exit. Richard walked over and locked the door as a safety precaution. He curiously watched through the window as Clara drove off quickly disappearing into the blackness of the night.

Weary from his chaotic encounter, Richard fell onto the sofa and he was on the brink of having an emotional moment when suddenly he heard the comforting voice of his daughter, Lesley.

"Daddy, are you okay?" Concern could be heard in Lesley's childlike voice.

Immediately, Richard motioned for Lesley to join him on the sofa. "Baby come sit down by daddy. I am fine, thanks to you. However,

Clara had to go away and unfortunately sweetheart you and your sister will never see Clara again. So, if she tries to come to your school, or to the house, that's when you and your sister should call me and 911. Lesley, do you understand what daddy is telling you? This is very important. I'm going to contact your school tomorrow and make them aware of what's going on." Richard spoke with decisiveness so his daughter would understand the seriousness of this situation.

"Yes daddy, I understand."

"Okay so let's get some sleep and I will talk to you and your sister more about what's going on in the morning, okay?"

"Okay daddy." Slowly, Lesley began making her way back to the bedroom, but suddenly she stopped and ran back to hug her daddy. Quickly grabbing Richard around his waist, she whispered. "Daddy I love you and I'm glad the angel woke me up and told me to go check on you before mean old Clara had a chance to hurt you."

Uncertainty appeared on Richard's weary face. "An angel?"

"Yes daddy. The angel told me to go check on you. At first, I thought she was the woman in the picture you showed me in your wallet. You told me that the lady in your wallet was mommy, and when I was four, mommy went to heaven, so I don't really know how mommy looked."

"Lesley sweetheart, you probably had a dream that an angel was talking to you."

"I guess so daddy maybe it was a dream, but the lady told me that she was our guardian angel and she said her name was, Carol.

Suddenly an expression of shock overshadowed Richard's face when Lesley spoke her mother's name. "Lesley, are you sure the angel said her name was Carol?"

"Yes daddy, I'm sure. Daddy, do you believe in angels?"

A glimpse of confusion continued to linger on Richard's face when his daughter asked this perplexing question. Since Carol's death, his faith in God or angels had not been on the top of his list. However, he did believe that if anyone was worthy of being an angel, it would be his beloved Carol.

"Yes Lesley. Anything is possible, anything."

CHAPTER 20

Dallas, TX, 1974

"Rachel are you sure moving out is a good idea?" Concern could be heard in the voice of Sandra.

"Yes I'm sure. Cousin Sandra, I think it's time my baby girl and me got out on our own. You have been so kind to allow us to live in your home over the past two years, but now I just want a little place for me to spread my wings, that's all. There is nothing you've done I just think it's time to go." Rachel tried to speak words of reassurance to her cousin, but she could tell from the poignant expression on Sandra's face, that she was not doing a good job.

"Rachel, why do you need a roommate? That girl Tracey is nothing but bad news I knew the first time I laid eyes on her that she was up to no good. I read her like a book and trust me, you don't need her staying with you and the baby. I don't understand why you brought her to Dallas with you anyway. When I came to Arkansas to bring you back with me, I had no idea that she was coming with you. I didn't like her then and I haven't changed my opinion about her to this day."

"Cousin Sandra, I just can't leave her hanging, she doesn't have a job, and she needs a place to stay so I suggested that she come and stay with me and April until she gets on her feet. Tracey is my friend and she has just fallen on hard times.

Don't worry about me and April, we'll be just fine." Rachel spoke with a calm voice hoping her demeanor provided comfort to her apprehensive cousin.

"Well, okay. If your mind is made up, I understand there is nothing I can say that will change your decision. I know because you have traits like me and your mother. We all are stubborn women so Rachel, sweetheart, if you need anything I'm just a phone call away, okay?"

"Thank you Cousin Sandra I so appreciate you, and I promise if April and I need anything we will contact you." Rachel was relieved that her cousin finally felt assured that she would be okay living on her own. Rachel still had a sense of great expectations for her future although she and her daughter's father had made the decision not to get married. They still were dating.

Now since Rachel had her own place, they would have the freedom to spend more time together. Who knows, perhaps one day the sparks would begin to ignite between the two of them and there could be a possibility they would tie the knot. Not only was Rachel dating her baby's daddy, but Tracey, her roommate was dating his brother, Jerry and from their actions, it appeared that those two were definitely in love.

Therefore, if Rachel didn't marry her daughter's father, perhaps her roommate would tie the knot with his brother, Jerry. Either way, Rachel would be happy and she was determined that nothing was going to ruin the happiness that she was feeling at that moment.

CHAPTER 21

One year had passed since Rachel made the decision to move out on her own. She was happy. Her daughter was happy and healthy, she had a good job working as a receptionist at a law firm, and her love for David was growing stronger each day. With each passing day, she anticipated David popping the big question.

The only thing causing her a little concern was David's brother, Jerry. There was something not right about this dude. Yes, he always appeared to be loving and considerate towards her roommate, and yes, he was always hanging around the apartment. If the truth was known, Rachel was even a little envious of him and Tracey's relationship in comparison to her and David's. However, Jerry never took Tracey any place. It was as if he was always sneaking around or as if he was trying to hide her from the outside world.

Rachel had met David and Jerry's parents on several occasions, but after a year of dating, Jerry had never introduced Tracey to his parents. The suspicion had become too intense, and Rachel vowed that she would confront Tracey when she came home from work that morning.

Tracey worked the night shift at a group home facility for mentally challenged individuals and Rachel knew how exhausted she would be. She also knew Tracey's routine. The moment she got home, her first desire was to take a long, hot shower, and go directly to bed. So the moment Rachel heard the door open, she confronted Tracey about this important matter.

"Tracey, I know you're tired, but I really need to talk to you about something that has been bothering me for a while. Could you give me a minute?" Rachel spoke with caution.

Demonstrating a nonchalant attitude, Tracey immediately reminded Rachel that she was too tired to talk. "Rachel, what it is? I am dead tired and you want to have a conversation about what? Okay, I'll give you five minutes so start talking!"

Hurriedly, Rachel began to speak. "I wanted to talk to you about Jerry!" Rachel didn't have the opportunity to begin the next sentence because Tracey immediately stopped her.

"What about Jerry?!" Tracey appeared agitated by Rachel's statement.

Rachel spoke with a rapid pace because her five minutes was quickly ticking down. "There's something odd about Jerry. I mean, you guys have dated for a year now and doesn't it seem odd that you have never met his parents? Doesn't it seem odd that you and Jerry never go out on a date? It's as if he's trying to hide you from the outside world."

"No, I wouldn't call his actions odd. I just think he's just waiting for the right time for me to meet his parents, and we don't go out on dates because he told me that he's trying to save money for some big event that's coming up." After speaking these words, a glimmer of happiness radiated upon Tracey's face because she had assumed that perhaps Jerry was saving money for their wedding. "Oh my Goodness! That's it!" she shouted with ecstatic excitement.

Rachel appeared confused by Tracey's sudden expression of blissfulness. "Tracey don't start getting any wild ideas that you and Jerry are getting married! I would hate to see you get your heart broken."

"Rachel, Jerry loves me and he would never break my heart! Now you on the other hand, you are the one who should be worried about your baby's daddy because you know he has been married before and if anybody's heart will get broken, it just might be yours. You know what I think Rachel? I think you're envious of me and Jerry's relationship! I see how you look at him when he comes over. You start rolling your eyes, and slamming things, acting like you're pissed off because he's here."

"Yes, I do get ticked off because all he does is come over here, screw you, and eat up all our food! Tell me Tracey, has he ever given you any money?"

Avoiding the question, Tracey glanced at her watch and spoke shrew words to Rachel. "Now your five minutes are up and this conversation is over!" As Tracey made her exit from the room, Rachel tried to make one last attempt to prove her point.

"Tracey just talk to Jerry because I still have a gut feeling that something is wrong!"

Yelling from behind the closed door of her bedroom, Tracey continued making harsh remarks to Rachel. "Rachel do me a favor, you take care of your damn business and stay out of mine!"

With those last words, Rachel vowed to herself that she would never interfere in Tracey's business again.

CHAPTER 22

"Are you sure you and April will be okay driving to Arkansas alone?" Rachel did not reply to David because six months ago he had agreed to accompany her to Arkansas for the Thanksgiving holiday. Nevertheless, for some odd reason, he suddenly changed his mind about going out of town with Rachel. "Rachel, please forgive me. Something came up and it's too late for me to make other plans. Baby, please don't leave angry."

Rachel managed to give David an easy smile. "I understand, but if you're really concerned, you would come with us."

"Baby I really wish I could go with you but as I said something came up and I can't back out of it now. And why isn't Tracey going with you?"

"She said Jerry wanted to spend some time with her before she went out of town. He told her that he was going to desperately miss her, so she's somewhere laid up with him and to night she's riding the bus to Arkansas. Isn't that stupid! Your brother has her wrapped around his little finger. He is so full of bull and she is so stupid if she believes his lies. David what is going on with your brother?"

When Rachel asked this question, she noticed a peculiar expression appear on David's face. "Baby, I'm sorry but I can't talk about this right now. Look, I think you should get on the road while you still have lots of daylight. You have a long drive ahead of you. Please call me when you arrive at your parent's house. I love you." With those last words, David kissed Rachel and his daughter good bye, got into his car, and drove off.

From David's reaction, Rachel knew that a storm was brewing on the horizon. She didn't know exactly what was going on, but a little voice inside of her head indicated that something terrible was about to happen.

Whatever drama that was about to take place, at least she and her daughter would not be in the midst of it all because they would be over three hundred miles away in the safety of her parent's home.

This was Rachel's first time driving to Arkansas alone. Since moving to Dallas she had driven home twice, but on each occasion Tracey had accompanied her and shared the three hour drive, which made the trip a piece of cake. Without Tracey, the drive was going to be long and dreary.

Rachel had been on the road for only an hour and she had stopped twice because she found herself becoming overwhelmed and exhausted.

Glancing in the back seat of the car at her daughter brought a sense of ease to Rachel's emotions. She knew she had precious cargo on board so she had to get herself together and persevere onward, but the longer she drove, the angrier she became each time Tracey crossed her mind. How could she be so selfish and only think of herself! She was probably lying up with that no good Jerry at this very moment. Rachel screamed loudly with anger. "Damn you Tracey!"

Rachel knew that she had to let go of the anger she was harboring within her heart towards Tracey and focus all her energy on getting her and April safely to her parent's house. At that moment, Rachel's thoughts were interrupted when she heard April's sweet little voice calling her name. "Mommy…I'm hungry."

Rachel was startled by April's actions because this was the first time she had heard her daughter speak a complete sentence. "April!

You spoke to mommy. Oh my goodness! Okay mommy will stop in a minute and get you something to eat."

The fact that April had spoken was the spark that was needed to uplift Rachel's spirits so without hesitation, she pulled into the next exit and stopped at McDonalds. She was going to treat her baby girl to whatever she wanted.

After spending thirty minutes enjoying a happy meal, a Big Mac and a strawberry shake with April, Rachel was on the road again. As of now, the trip was beginning to be quite pleasant and after driving for two more hours, Rachel and April arrived at her parent's house. With a quick toot of her horn, the doors of her parent's house immediately flew open and without hesitation, Rachel saw her parents, and her sister quickly emerge from inside. Rachel and April were greeted with loving hugs and kisses. Yes, this was going to be a wonderful Thanksgiving holiday.

CHAPTER 23

Sunday came and it was time for Rachel and April to leave Arkansas, and as always, departure was a sad occasion. When Rachel embraced her father, he suddenly started crying. When she embraced her mom she burst into tears also. "Sweetheart I'm going to miss you and April so much. Now you take care of yourself and my sweet little granddaughter." Her statement was spoken with love and sincerity.

"Now you drive carefully going back home and if you get tired, pull over and rest awhile." Rachel was aware of the concern in the voice of her father.

"Daddy, the drive will be much easier going back because I'm picking Tracey up from her parent's house. She came down on the bus Thursday night, so she's riding back with me and April, and she will help do some of the driving."

"That's great because when you told me that you were driving down here alone, I was really worried about you. But, the angels watched over you and little April, and brought you two safely home to us. Thank you Jesus!" Rachel's dad was not timid about expressing gratitude for God's blessings over his daughter and granddaughter.

Twenty minutes later, Rachel and April had arrived at the home of Tracey's parents. Tracey was sitting on the front steps impatiently waiting for Rachel. She quickly rushed toward the car and told Rachel she wanted the first option of driving. This was fine with Rachel because she felt relieved that she didn't have to drive back to Dallas alone.

For over an hour, there was complete silence between Tracey and Rachel until Rachel finally broke the ice and inquired about Tracey's holiday with her family. "It was really nice. It was great seeing my parents again and of course we had so much food!"

"I know what you mean we had a lot of food too! I jokingly asked my mom was she planning on feeding a football team or what! So before I left, I fixed about ten plastic containers filled with everything she prepared. I'm gonna eat left over's until there is nothing left over!" Rachel's statement was followed by a humorous laugh of gaiety.

It still appeared that Tracey was not in a good mood, so Rachel continued the conversation with an attempt to get to the core of what was going on with her friend. "Tracey is everything okay?"

With a tone of exasperation, Tracey replied to Rachel's question. "Yes… I mean… I'm not sure. Jerry and I had a big argument."

Tracey's answer heightened Rachel's curiosity. "You had an argument about what?"

"Well… I asked Jerry about the discussion that you and I had. You know why I've never met his parents, and why we rarely go out on a date. The only place he takes me is to that little hole in the wall club down the street. Rachel when I started asking him questions, he blew up like a wild man! He started cursing me, and talking to me like I was a dog and he told me that if I didn't like what was going on, then he would dump me! I had never seen this side of Jerry before. So the minute I get home I'm going to call Jerry because he has some explaining to do! Tracey's voice trembled with anger.

Rachel didn't know how to reply to her friend. After all, she had made a vow to herself that she would never interfere in Tracey's business again. Therefore, to break the ice between them she decided to release Tracey from her driving duties. "Tracey, you can pull over at the next rest stop so I can check April's pull up, then I'll take over and drive us into Dallas."

The next rest stop was only five miles away so, Tracey pulled into the rest stop, and Rachel took over driving. After listening to Tracey's complaint concerning Jerry, Rachel reflected on a statement she had made prior to arriving in Arkansas concerning a storm that was about to take place. After listening to Tracey, Rachel definitely knew that the storm had already arrived.

CHAPTER 24

*N*ightfall was slowly casting a dark shadow over Dallas when Rachel and Tracey made their entrance into the city. The moment the car stopped, Tracey immediately jumped out and ran into the apartment to call Jerry. She was in Arkansas for four days and Jerry had not called her, so you can imagine the frustration Tracey was feeling.

Rachel went inside the apartment and placed little April on the floor and went back outside to remove her suitcase. Then to her surprise, she saw David driving into the parking lot. "David what are you doing here?"

"I wanted to be here when you and April returned home. Did you have a good time? How was your family?"

Rachel didn't know what was going on with David because his behavior was extremely erratic. "David everything went fine. We had a great time, thanks for calling to make sure April and I made it home safely. David could you please tell me what's going on?"

"Rachel, I love you and April and there is nothing that I wouldn't do for you two." David walked closer to Rachel and gently took her hand. "Here let me carry some of those things inside for you. Is my baby girl inside?"

"Yes, she's inside with Tracey." When Rachel mentioned Tracey's name, it caused David to freeze in his steps, and an expression of exasperation was reflected upon his face. "David what's wrong with you?"

Before David could answer Rachel, he was confronted by Tracey. Desperation could be heard in her voice. "David, have you heard from Jerry?"

"Tracey, you haven't talked to Jerry?" A glimmer of what appeared to be fear reflected upon David's face. "Jerry promised he would talk to you before you went to Arkansas."

"Talk to me about what?" Tracey expressed confusion on her face. "David what was Jerry going to talk to me about?" Rage was heard in Tracey's voice.

David was taken off guard by Tracey's question and at that moment, he was filled with anger towards his brother because he had not spoken to Tracey as he promised. Slowly making his way inside the apartment David asked to use the phone. "Could I use your phone?" David asked with a tone of irritation. "I think you should talk to Jerry about what's going on."

"No you can't use the phone! You tell me what's going on with Jerry right now!" Tracey was in David's face, and at this point, her demeanor had reached the boiling point.

"David if you know something about Jerry please tell her!" Tracey yelled with a sense of annoyance.

With the assumption that if he did not speak David knew that he was going to have a serious problem with Tracey, so he quickly blurted out the truth. "Jerry got married Saturday night."

Both Tracey and Rachel were dumbfounded by the statement that David had just made and with mouths wide open, it took a few seconds before either of them could speak. Slowly Tracey took a seat on the sofa, finally finding the words to speak. "Married! David don't play with me because I'm not in the mood for this foolishness!" Tracey hissed with fury.

With a look of dread and defeat, David continued. "Tracey, I am telling you the truth. Jerry got married on Saturday and he was supposed to talk to you about this. I told him that what he was doing was wrong."

"You mean the fact that he was two-timing Tracey? Isn't that what you should be saying? No, it was not right it was malicious! It was heartless! David, I can't believe that you were a part of this mess!" Rachel was livid with David because he had gone along with Jerry's scheme. "How could you come over here every day, and look Tracey in the face, knowing that your brother was going to betray her? What kind of person are you?" "Tracey I'm so sorry." Remorse could be heard in David's voice. "What was I suppose to do? After all, Jerry is my brother! You will never know how many times I wanted to tell you what was going on. I wanted to tell Rachel what was happening. But I just couldn't. I was a coward and I didn't want to get in the middle of this mess and I definitely didn't want Rachel to get involved and this is the main reason why I didn't say anything."

"David please just get out of here because I don't believe anything you're saying right now. Who knows, you're probably plotting to do the same thing to me." With those spoken words, Rachel walked over to the door and held it open for David to make his exit.

"Rachel..." David attempted to make one last stand before making his exit, but Rachel's reply was when she slammed the door in David's face.

CHAPTER 25

Tracey ran out of the apartment. Dazed and incoherent would best describe her frame of mind as she listlessly wandered the dark streets of Dallas. For hours, she tried to understand why Jerry would hurt her so badly. Unanswered questions kept spinning around and around inside her tormented head. It was as if she was on a merry-go-round and couldn't get off. "Why Jerry, Why!" Tracey cried out in agony.

Her screams of agony were heard by individuals passing in the night on the street, and she was confronted face to face by glaring eyes of strangers who perhaps assumed that she was an out of control lunatic. However, she didn't give a damn about their assumptions because the pain that she was harboring inside her heart was no comparison to what people thought.

Peering through swollen eyes blurred from hours of crying, Tracey noticed the club, The Blue Lagoon, in the distance. It was where she and Jerry would go whenever they went out. Tracey took a seat at the bar and asked the bartender for a double shot of scotch. As the bartender began pouring the drink, he recognized Tracey's face. "So where's your boyfriend tonight?" Sammy the bartender was not aware that Jerry had gotten married. "Oh, so I guess you two had a fight or something, right?"

Tracey did not reply because she thought Sammy was being amusing. She was under the assumption that everyone, except her, knew about Jerry's marriage. Without replying to Sammy's question, Tracey requested a second round and without hesitation, Sammy honored her wishes. However, after the third round of drinks, Sammy wanted to know how Tracey would pay for the drinks. By now, Tracey could barely stand, nor speak in a normal manner. Slurring her words, she informed Sammy to put it on her tab.

"You don't have a tab!" Sammy rudely yelled. "And you're going to pay for these drinks, or you'll be waiting on tables for the rest of the night!"

Tracey began screaming, stumbling, and crying at the same time. She was yelling in Sammy's face, screaming and shouting like a mad woman. "I'm not waiting on tables put the drinks on my tab! Or, if you want, you can put it on your boy Jerry's tab! You know Jerry, don't you Sammy? Jerry is the fool who got married on me Saturday night! Were you at the wedding?"

Sammy appeared bewildered by Tracey's outburst. "No, I wasn't at the wedding and I didn't know Jerry got married. You're drunk, little girl, and if you pay me my money and get out of here right now, I won't call the police on you. So don't push your luck. Give me my money get the hell out of here now!

"Sammy, I'll take care of her." This familiar voice grasped the attention of Tracey, and when she turned around, she stared into the kind face of Rachel's cousin, Sandra. Reaching into her purse, Sandra took out a fifty-dollar bill and quickly placed it into Sammy's hand, and made a hasty remark. "You should be ashamed of yourself, threatening to call the police on this poor child. Can't you see she's going through something?" Reaching for Tracey's hand, and with the assistance of a nice couple, Tracey was escorted out of the club. "Come on baby, let's get you home," Sandra spoke with empathy.

Once in the car and too embarrassed to face Sandra, Tracey turned her head and stared out the window glaring into the darkness. "How did you find me?" She inquired with a sluggish tone.

"Rachel told me what that idiot, Jerry, did to you and she told me that sometimes he would take you to a club that was about five blocks down the street. She couldn't remember the name of the club, so, I just started driving, and The Blue Lagoon, was the only club, five blocks from the apartment. I assumed this was the right one, and it appears that I got here just in time to save you from a beat down."

"Thanks, Cousin Sandra. I was acting like a drunken fool! I'm just so hurt and I don't know what I'm going to do without Jerry." Despair could be heard in Tracey's voice.

"Girl you're going to live, laugh and someday you're going to love again. What you're going through right now, I bet half of the women in Dallas have experienced the same situation at least once in their lifetime. Truthfully, I've been betrayed by a man at least twice. The first time I was betrayed, I have to admit that I was hurt, but I learned that you can't stay in a rut for too long because you will get depressed. So, you gotta pull yourself up and start living again. You gotta move on because Jerry has moved on and he's not coming back. He's married now… understand? He has a wife! Tracey take my advice and you do the same. Move on, because Jerry ain't the only man walking around on this earth!"

"How do you move on?" Tracey asked waiting for a reply.

"You ask God to help you let go of Jerry and you start focusing on what's best for you. You allow yourself to heal before you get involved in another relationship. Don't try to replace Jerry with somebody else. Take time to get to know yourself before you bring someone else into the equation. Do you understand?"

Tracey took a long deep breath and let out a weary sigh. "Yes Cousin Sandra, I understand."

When Sandra and Tracey arrived at the apartment, Rachel immediately opened the door. Quickly rushing over to Tracey, Rachel expressed emotions of concern and embraced Tracey. "I was so worried about you, are you okay?" She asked and anxiety could be heard in her voice.

To Rachel's surprise, Tracey quickly pushed her away, and harsh words were spoken. "I'm fine but Rachel I will never forgive you because you knew Jerry was getting married. Didn't you?"

Tracey appeared to be deranged and her accusations were inaccurate, because Rachel had no idea that Jerry was getting married. "Tracey you can't be serious! How could I have known that Jerry was getting married?" Rachel replied in amazement.

"David probably told you and you kept it a secret from me!" Tracey yelled. Anger and hostility could be heard in her voice. "But that's okay because I'll get you for this! How could you betray me like this?"

"Tracey listen to me! I didn't betray you because I didn't know that Jerry was getting married! David never told me anything! You gotta believe me!"

"Liar! You're a liar Rachel and I'm going to get you for betraying me. You won't know when or where, but I'll get you!" Tracey's demeanor was now expressing extreme hostility.

Sandra, was extremely concerned by the conversation between Tracey and Rachel and she decided that it was time to break up what was about to become a chaotic situation. "Tracey, that's enough! If Rachel said she didn't know that Jerry was getting married, then she's telling you the truth. This is your best friend. How could you think that she would betray you? The only person that you should be upset with is that fool Jerry. But at some point, you're going to have to find it in your heart to forgive him too. So, girl get off you high horse and apologize to Rachel, and as I told you in the car, let this nonsense go and move on with your life!"

Sandra's words were harsh and to the point.

However, Tracey did not apologize to Rachel she angrily rushed into her bedroom and locked the door.

Rachel appeared hurt and confused from the implications of her roommate. "Cousin Sandra, why would Tracey think I would betray her?"

"Rachel, right now she's confused and hurt but honey if I were you, until things blow over, I would sleep with one eye open. This thing with Jerry has put a whammy on her and if she is not careful, she could have a nervous breakdown. From what I just saw, I'm concerned about the safety of you and April. I think it would be a good idea if you and April came over and stayed with me for a while until Tracey gets herself together." Sandra's voice expressed remorse and concern for Rachel and April.

"Thank you Cousin Sandra but I can't abandon Tracey at a crucial time like this. She really needs my help now! She has nobody but me and if I leave her now, I would be doing the same thing that Jerry did to her. No, I'm going to stay here and help get her through this mess. I know she would do the same thing for me."

"Okay Rachel if you insist but be careful and watch your back. You call me if you need anything, okay?" Sandra spoke to Rachel with a manner of precaution.

After Sandra, left the apartment once again, Rachel tried to reach out to Tracey but she didn't receive a positive response. So, at 1 am Rachel decided to crawl into bed next to April to get some sleep, because tomorrow was a workday. She was so worn out from the tense occurrences that had taken place that evening and the moment her head hit the pillow, she immediately fell asleep.

At 4 am Tracey made an exit from her bedroom and went into Rachel's bedroom. As she gazed upon Rachel's motionless sleeping body, anger consumed Tracey's mind. At that moment, she hated

Rachel because she was convinced that Rachel knew about Jerry's marriage, and she had decided that she was going to make Rachel pay for the pain that she was suffering. Quietly, Tracey tiptoed closer to Rachel's bed, and from behind her back, she slowly brought forth the .357 Magnum that Rachel's father had given her when she moved to Dallas. Rachel disclosed the whereabouts of the gun to Tracey in the event of an unwanted intruder. The gun was in the apartment to give them a sense of safety since they were two single girls living alone in the big city. Now it appeared that the very weapon that was to be used for her protection was about to be used as a sentence of death against Rachel and her daughter.

Tracey raised the cold black barrel of the gun downwards until it was aimed directly at Rachel's head. Tracey's trembling hand held the gun tightly as her right finger slowly began pulling the trigger.

CHAPTER 26

Tracey's hand began to shake with an uncontrollable, vigorous movement and tears began streaming down her face. "What am I doing?" She quietly murmured to herself as she quickly, lowered the gun to her side. Seconds later, the phone started ringing and swiftly, she made her exit from the bedroom. Fortunately, Rachel and little April remained sleeping in a quiet slumber. With a quick rush, she grabbed the phone in her bedroom.

At first, Tracey's voice was quiet and listless, but the moment she recognized the voice of the person on the phone, her voice echoed to a higher pitch expressing rage, and hurt all entangled together. It took a moment for her to let the name of this person roll from her quivering lips. Her anger escalated. "Jerry, why in hell are you calling me? Haven't you done enough damage to my heart?" she yelled with fury.

"Tracey, I'm so sorry. I wanted to tell you, but I couldn't." Jerry's voice was trembling.

"Jerry. I'm hanging up right now, and never in my lifetime do I ever want to hear your voice again! Do you understand?" Tracey's words were drenched with rage and unforgiveness.

"Tracey please don't hang up! The guilt that I am carrying around is driving me crazy! Please, just give me five minutes to explain." Jerry pleaded.

"Five minutes, Jerry! Tracey shouted with extreme anger.

"I got this girl pregnant and her father told me that if I didn't marry her, he would kill me! Tracey I believed him! Her old man is a gangster he's one of biggest drug dealers in Dallas. I know for certain, some guys who are now six feet under because of this dude. Tracey, I did what I had to do. Baby I am so sorry, but please know that I will always love you, but Tracey I had no choice except to marry this girl."

"Did Rachel know about your wedding?"

"What?" Jerry asked.

"I asked you, did Rachel know about your wedding?"

"No, she didn't know about my wedding. I made David promise that he wouldn't say anything to Rachel about the wedding."

"Okay, that's all I wanted to know. Your five minutes are up. Jerry, you and your wife have a wonderful life, and please, lose my phone number and don't ever call me again!" With those last words, Tracey hung up the phone.

A few weeks later, Tracey decided to move out of the apartment with Rachel. She knew David would continue seeing Rachel and she didn't want any reminders of his brother. Therefore, in an effort to avoid David, she moved out.

The relationship between David and Rachel blossomed into a beautiful love affair and within a year, they were married and four years later another baby girl was added to their family.

However, there are times when love does not last forever, and the marriage between David and Rachel ended in divorce three years later.

Life went on for Rachel and she remarried a second time and had a beautiful son, but three years later once again she found herself in divorce court. She remarried a third time but five years later, this marriage ended in divorce as well. David also remarried, but unfortunately, within a year, he passed away from a massive heart attack.

Tracey and Rachel's friendship ended and Rachel had no idea what happened to her best friend. The memories of both David, and Tracey would always remain within Rachel's heart, but time quickly continued to slip into the future, and she anticipated a bright, happy future, which perhaps someday would include the man of her dreams.

CHAPTER 27

Fort Collins, Colorado

Six months after his turbulent marriage to Clara ended Richard went on a rampage in search of a new mother for his children. Wife number three was a woman named Jenny Wilson who he met at his office Christmas party. He dated Jenny one week and married her without knowing anything about her past.

Three months later, Richards' joint checking account with Jenny was overdrawn on several occasions. He also noticed that items had started disappearing from his house. His gold watch that was given to him by Carol for his birthday was missing. His gold chain and his camera were missing as well. When he questioned Jenny about the checking account and about the disappearance of the other items, she had no answers to satisfy Richard's questions.

Weeks went by. One afternoon Richard took ill and went home early, and the truth about what was going on was finally revealed. When he went into the bedroom, he discovered Jenny snorting cocaine. "What are you doing?" He was outraged at Jenny's behavior.

Caught in the act, Jenny was startled by Richards' unexpected appearance, and she attempted to hide the drugs but her efforts were unsuccessful because the evidence of white cocaine covered Jenny's nose. "Richard, what are you doing home so early?" Her voice trembled in a shocking tone.

"Now I know why our account is always overdrawn, and why my watch and my camera came up missing. You're a damn drug addict and you pawned my things, didn't you!" Richard was outraged, and he grabbed Jenny and pulled her closely. His voice echoed throughout the room as he screamed and shouted into Jenny's face. Jenny, felt Richard's hot saliva showering into her face and she trembled with fear, assuming that perhaps Richard was at the breaking point and his next step would be to physically attack her.

"Get your things and get out of my house!" Yes, Richards' anger had escalated to its highest peak but he had never hit a woman before and he wasn't about to start now. However, if he had to look at Jenny a minute longer, perhaps there would be some disastrous results.

With haste, Jenny started gathering her things from the bathroom, the dresser, and the closet and she threw them into a suitcase. Richard grabbed her by the arms and escorted her down stairs. Crying and shaking like a terrified animal, Jenny held tightly to Richards's shirt and began begging for his forgiveness. "Richard, please forgive me, don't throw me out, I just need help. I'll go to rehab I'll do whatever you want me to do, but please don't throw me out!"

Richard showed no remorse from the hysterical pleads of this woman. In fact, he became even more angered when he took a moment to reflect on the hurt and pain he had endured when he was shafted by his ex-wife Clara and the nerve of this woman to do the exact same thing. "No Jenny it's over, get out of my house!" With a slight push, Jenny was outside, and Richard quickly slammed the door in her tear stained face.

For a brief moment, Richard sat in solitude and fixed his eyes on a picture of his daughters. How was he going to explain to them what had happened between he and Jenny? He closed his eyes and tried to think of some creative story to tell his girls. Nothing came to his mind except to just tell them the truth. His girls were of age now, and they would understand.

Richard decided that he would give himself a break from marriage and he would try dating instead of putting a ring on a woman's finger. A few months later, he starting dating a woman he met one night when he and several guys from his office were out on the town. Sarah Roswell caught Richard's attention when she deliberately strolled over to the bar where he was sitting and took a seat next to him. She was wearing a very revealing, low cut red dress that left little to the imagination. "Hey soldier could you buy a girl a drink?"

Turning, Richard faced this strange woman and replied to her request. "Sure, what are you drinking?"

"A glass of red wine would be great!"

After that night, Richard and Sarah were inseparable and after months of dating Richard was sure that she was the one and he was in the process of asking Sarah to marry him but he reconsidered after having a frank conversation with his younger brother.

"Richard is love or lust the main reasons why you keep marrying all these women?" his brother Daniel asked when he came to visit Richard one summer.

"It could possibly be both." Richard replied with a mischievous sigh. "However, you know I have these two little girls, and they need a mother. I mean, it's difficult taking care of girls."

Richard's brother looked confused. "So you're telling me that the real reason you keep marrying these estranged women, is to find a mother for your children?"

"Yes, that's the main motive behind me marrying these women." Richard replied with sincerity.

"Wow! I hate to tell you this big brother, but that was the most selfish thing I have ever heard you say. You don't need anybody to help you raise your daughters! It's not like they were infants, your daughters are what, twelve and ten? Come on man, basically they can take care of themselves, you just need to be around to financially provide for them, protect them and do what you're supposed to do as a father. I mean, your mentality of having a woman around, in my opinion is just a cop out!" Daniel gave Richard his honest opinion concerning the situation.

Richard was not pleased with his brother's opinion and suggested that he stay out of his business. Richard did propose to Sarah, but she turned him down. "Richard we've had a blast together, but settling down with you is just completely out of the question. I'm having too much fun letting men "wine, and dine" me and of course I love when they put a little extra change in my purse, as well. Therefore, you tell me, why would I want to be tied down to one man?"

Yes, Richard was somewhat heartbroken, from his break up, but he did recover from Sarah's little slap in the face and a year later he got himself into another quandary and married wife number four. Private Stephanie Jenkins was a woman whom he had recruited three years prior. After basic training, Stephanie was stationed in Germany for two years and after completing her tour of duty overseas, she arrived back in the states and was assigned to Richard's base in Colorado.

The first time Richard laid eyes on Stephanie, it was love at first sight and they started dating. Two months later, they flew to Vegas and got married. Six months later Richard would discover that Stephanie was not fond of his children. The constant fighting and hostility between his wife and daughters was never ending and fearing for the safety of his daughters became a reality. Therefore, unfortunately, Richard made the decision that it would be in the best interest of everyone that he ended his marriage to Stephanie.

"Richard, like I told you my brother, Leave these women alone! You don't need to find a mama for your girls! You're all they need."

Once again, Richard's brother tried to give him wise advice. However, would he listen this time? Only time would reveal the truth.

CHAPTER 28

Once again, Richard did not listen to his brother's words of wisdom because one year later he married wife number five, a young woman named Veronica Peters who was a nurse at the VA hospital. On his routine visit at the hospital, he spotted Veronica coming out of the coffee shop. For Veronica, it was love at first sight. She confessed her love to Richard in a very bold manner, but once again, Richard's one and only motive was to get a mother for his daughters. The attempt was a successful one and after six months of dating, under the false pretenses of his heart, Richard confessed his love for Veronica so he could make her wife number five, Mrs. Richard McWilliams.

Not everyone was pleased with Richard's decision to marry again. His father was especially against the decision. "Richard all you're doing is complicating your life and the lives of your daughters. What you should do, son, is marry your children and start leaving these women out of the equation. Mark my words if you don't listen to me one day you will regret these decisions you have made about marrying all these women."

However, Richard did not listen to the wisdom of his father because at the time he didn't understand what his father meant when he said, "you should marry your children." Therefore, Richard carried out his plans to marry Veronica.

To the marriage, three children were born, two boys and a daughter. Now Richard had the responsibility of five children in his household, with the occasional visit from his son Richard Jr, who lived with his in laws. As the years slipped quickly into the future, it appeared that Richard had once again found a love in comparison to what he once shared with his late wife Carol.

On this particular day, Richard was excited because of the special surprise he had planned for their fifth wedding anniversary. Unknown to Veronica, he had hired an overnight babysitter because he had made reservations at the Chate La'Rue, which was Veronica's favorite restaurant. He also made reservations at Cliff Mount Ridge, a small ski lodge nestled in the beautiful snowy mountains of Denver. Excitement was in Richard's voice when he called Veronica to confirm the time she would leave work. "Veronica the moment you get home, I need you to go in, take a shower, and put on your best dress because I've planned a really special evening for our anniversary. Oh, you should pack a small overnight bag as well."

Exhaustion was clear in Veronica's voice. She had worked a twelve-hour shift at the hospital and her plans were to go home, take a long hot bath, and climb into bed. Going out on a date with Richard was not in her equation. "Richard that sounds great, but I am exhausted! We had seven emergencies at the hospital tonight and I have been on my feet for twelve hours. I know it's our anniversary, but when I get home my plans are to soak in the tub, and afterwards crawl into bed."

Richard was extremely disappointed with Veronica's answer, and he was at a loss for words. He didn't know how to reply to her statement. For months now, he had made plans and tedious preparations in order to have a memorable anniversary. Now it appeared that his plans were going to be shattered.

"Richard, did you hear what I said? I would prefer to stay at home tonight." Veronica spoke with determination.

"Yes I heard you. If that's what you want, then we will stay home."

Immediately hanging up the phone, Richard called the restaurant, and the lodge to cancel both reservations and he also called the babysitter to inform her that her services would not be needed for the night. "So much for trying to surprise her." He muffled with a short sigh that displayed disappointment.

When Veronica arrived home, Richard's disappointment somewhat subsided once he laid eyes on his wife. He could tell that she really was exhausted. Her face appeared drained from the activities that had taken place at the hospital. It appeared that her duties of being head nurse were taking a toll on her both physically and mentally. Therefore, Richard prepared a hot bubble bath to help soothe Veronica's tired body. When he led her into the bathroom, he also had candles around the bathtub that gave off a scent of jasmine and a bright glow from the candles illuminated the bathroom.

There was also a glass of red wine sitting on the edge of tub to help with Veronica's relaxation process.

The gratitude in Veronica's eyes warmed Richard's heart. He suddenly felt embarrassed because of his reaction when Veronica told him she was too exhausted to go out to dinner. Now he understood that there would be occasions when his plans would not go his way, but his reward was the satisfaction that appeared in Veronica's eyes. Yes, dinner and the lodge would have been wonderful, but to Veronica, a simple gesture such as a bubble bath, candles, and a glass of wine had made the biggest impression on her.

CHAPTER 29

"Richard, I don't understand! Why would you volunteer to go way across the country to take a position as an instructor? You'll be away for six months and I'll be stuck here with all these kids!" Veronica was livid after learning that Richard was transferring to Savannah, Georgia. "Richard, there is no way I can work ten and twelve hour shifts at the hospital, come home and take care of six kids. I just can't do this anymore!"

"Veronica, I've already received my orders, and everything has been arranged. I'm leaving in two days. I can't back out now!"

"Richard why didn't you discuss this with me? You never asked my opinion about going to Savannah! How could you be so inconsiderate? I need you here!" Veronica was pacing back and forth, swinging her arms, expressing anger and frustration concerning Richard's decision.

Richard reached for Veronica's hand, but she quickly withdrew it with an angry jerk. "Veronica, they offered me twice the salary that I'm making here at the base. We can always use the money. Baby, be reasonable, we have six kids to support! I'm only thinking about our future, and the future of our children. This could be extra money we could put back for the kids education."

"I can't do this Richard, I'm already on the edge now with work, and coming home to help with homework, and cooking dinner and don't mention trying to keep the house clean." Veronica walked over and frantically began picking up shoes and toys that the kids had left lying around. "Look at all this stuff! I can't even keep the house clean because of these kids! They are out of control! Richard, please don't leave me like this, I can't do this alone!" Veronica's request was of desperation.

"Veronica I can't stay. I'll see if it's in our budget to hire someone to help you out sometimes with the kids, but I can't stay." Richard's mind would not be deterred, even with Veronica's heart wrenching appeal for him not to abandon her.

Two months after Richard's departure to Savannah, Veronica suffered a nervous breakdown and was admitted to the hospital for a few weeks of rest, and Richard had to return to Fort Collins. "I should have listened to her." His voice was somber, showing signs of regret because he didn't take heed to Veronica's request. "Doctor Beasley, she told me she wouldn't be able to handle the pressure of working and taking care of the kids."

"Richard, she's going to be fine, but is there any way you could remain here until she gets better and then resume your duties in Savannah? If you like, I could speak with your commanding officer on your behalf."

"Thanks doctor Beasley, I'll stay for a few days, but after that, I'm going back to Savannah. There's one thing my dad always taught my brothers and me, is to always finish what we started. I have four months to complete my duties in Savannah, and that's what I'm going to do." Richard's voice was full of fortitude.

Doctor Beasley was not pleased with Richard's reply and considered it to be a lack of empathy for Veronica. "Richard my main objective is the wellbeing of my patient. And right now, I think you're being somewhat selfish." Doctor Beasley's tone was firm with a hint of anger. "Are you okay? I ask this question because for some reason, you're not expressing any signs of empathy for your wife. What's going on Richard?"

"Doctor Beasley, I appreciate your concern, but I'll handle my own affairs." With those sharp words, Richard walked away, ending the conversation. He remained with his family for three days afterwards he returned to Savannah.

As the months passed, Veronica's condition improved somewhat. With the assistance of a family member, who came to her rescue to assist with the children for a few weeks, she was able to return to her position at the hospital, but still things were not back to normal in the household. After her family member left, once again, things became chaotic in the home, but the worst was yet to come.

One afternoon Veronica's co-worker, Joanna Carson, made a surprised visit to the home. The first thing that shocked Joanna to the core was the fact that she was greeted at the door by an eight year old. "Sweetie is your mom at home?" she inquired with curiosity.

"Yes ma'am she's in her room asleep," the small voice replied.

Once inside, Joanna was appalled by the deplorable conditions of the house.

The first thing that almost knocked her off her feet was an undesirable, foul smell that consumed her nostrils. Then she noticed toys and clothes lying everywhere on the floor. There were dishes stacked in the kitchen sink, and bits of food was splattered on the floor. In addition, out of curiosity, she opened the door to the utility room, and she could not see the washer and dryer because a tall stack of smelly clothing was covering both appliances.

However, what was really hammering inside Joanna's mind was the fact that a child opened the door, allowing a complete stranger to enter into the house. "God, what if I would have been a murderer or a kidnapper!" she angrily murmured to herself. The thought of what if made her shiver with fear. "Sweetie could you take me to your mom?"

Joanna spoke in a concerned tone, but anger began to consume her mind as she followed this child down the hallway. She was trying to process the fact that a small child had just allowed a total stranger to enter the house.

After the child opened the door, Joanna saw Veronica sleeping soundly amongst a pile of pillows and at least two blankets. Standing over her, Joanna called Veronica's name twice with a loud shout before getting a response.

Peering through sleepy matted eyes, Veronica appeared shocked to see Joanna standing by her bedside. "Joanna, what are you doing here?" she asked with a slurring voice of fatigue.

"Veronica, I've called your phone at least six times because you were scheduled to work Angie Thomas's shift. Her shift started two hours ago. Therefore, when we didn't hear from you, Doctor Reed asked if anyone knew where you lived, so I told him that I did. So he told me to come by to make sure that everything was okay." Peering into Veronica's alarmed yet sleepy eyes Joanna asked the curious question. "Is everything okay Veronica?"

Ignoring the question, in a panic, Veronica quickly leaped from the bed. "On my god!" she vigorously shouted. "Joanna, I'm so sorry, I overslept, and I turned my phone off last night because it kept ringing late into the night. This woman kept calling my number apparently, she had the wrong number. In addition, I guess I turned my alarm off too! Joanna, give me ten minutes and I'll be ready to go."

Veronica made a mad dash into the bathroom. "Veronica, what about your daughter? Who's going to stay with her?" Concern was heard in Joanna's voice.

"She'll have to stay here alone for about an hour the other kids will be home from school at 4pm."

"Are you sure she'll be okay?" Joanna inquired with concern.

"Yes she'll be fine." Veronica was now making her way out of the bedroom to where Joanna was standing. "Joanna, you can go now and I'll be right behind you, I just need to speak to Tonya for a moment."

Joanna walked out of the house slowly because she was torn with trying to decide if she should confront Veronica about the unusual circumstances that she had witnessed. She was struggling with the unsafe and unsanitary conditions of Veronica's house. These images continually permeated her mind. Should she get involved in Veronica's affairs? She couldn't make such a hasty judgment at that moment, but she did know that her main concern was the safety and the wellbeing of the children. "If something happened to those children because I kept my mouth shut I would never forgive myself. I have to tell somebody, but who?

"Richard," she spoke quietly to herself. "I need to find a way to get in touch with Richard. I am sure he doesn't know what's going on here. How can I contact him? I know he is in Savannah, but where? I can't ask Veronica for Richard's phone number, this would only arouse her suspicious, and I don't want to alert her as to why I'm calling Richard."

Then it was as if a light bulb went off inside Joanna's head. "Doctor Beasley, he would know how to contact Richard." The moment Joanna arrived at the hospital, she immediately made her way towards Doctor Beasley's office but she was stopped by his receptionist.

"Joanna, what are you doing here?" Paulette, the receptionist inquired. Paulette and Joanna had been friends for many years, and she was surprised to see her friend in the office.

"Hi Paulette, everything is fine, but I really need to see doctor Beasley for just a split second."

"Is it really that important?" Paulette asked with a hint of curiosity in her voice.

"Yes, it's really important." Joanna whispered in a low discreet voice.

"Okay go on back." Paulette opened the door and motioned for Joanna to enter. "Go into his office, because he's with a patient at the moment, but the second he comes out, I'll let him know you're here."

"Thanks Paulette." Joanna replied with gratitude.

Five minutes later, Doctor Beasley entered his office. "Joanna, what a surprise, what can I do for you?" he asked with inquisitiveness.

"Doctor Beasley, I'm sorry to barge in like this, but I really would like to speak to you about Veronica McWilliams. She is your patient, isn't she?"

"Yes she is. But what's going on with Veronica?"

"She's the head nurse on my floor and I consider her a friend as well. However, something odd is going on with her. Everyone on her floor has noticed a change in her personality since her mental melt down a few months ago." Joanna spoke with concern.

"Yes, I spoke to Richard about her condition before he went back to Savannah, and I assured him that Veronica would be fine. As a doctor, I have my limitations. I do what is medically needed, but the rest is out of my hands."

"I understand doctor Beasley but today, I went to Veronica's house and I witnessed some disturbing conditions. In my opinion, the children who live in that house need immediate attention and quite honestly, I fear for their safety. So I'm here because I thought perhaps you should contact Richard because I believe he should know about what's going on."

"What did you see Joanna?"

"Doctor Beasley, I really don't want to tell all of Veronica's business, but trust me, Richard should make plans to come back here as soon as possible."

"Okay, from what I'm hearing in your voice, I believe I should contact Richard and inform him of what's going on. So, let me take care of my patients and I will give Richard a call. Thank you Joanna for making me aware of what's going on."

"Thank you Doctor Beasley." She sighed with relief. Joanna left Doctor Beasley's office with a sense of accomplishment. She didn't know what the outcome of Veronica's dilemma would be, and she did feel empathy for Veronica, but her main concern was the well-being of the children and perhaps her involvement would in some way prevent any endangerment to the children.

CHAPTER 30

Fort Collins, Colorado

"Richard, this is Doctor Beasley."
"Yes Doctor Beasley, what's going on?"
"Richard when will you return to Fort Collins?"
"I will return tomorrow."
"That's good to hear. Have you spoken to Veronica recently?"
"Yes, I spoke with her last week. She and the kids are doing fine. Doctor Beasley, is there any particular reason why you called me?"
"Yes and no. I have only spoke with Veronica twice since she was released from the hospital. Once for her checkup and once just passing in the hallway here at the hospital, and I agree, she was fine at that time.
However, from what I have learned today from a reliable source, it appears that perhaps Veronica has had somewhat of a setback. Richard I cannot confirm that this is true, but as I said, I did receive some information from a reliable source, that is causing me some concern. So, my question is, do you want me to speak to Veronica to see what's going on or would you prefer that I let it go, and wait until you return home?"
"Thanks Doctor Beasley for your concern but, I'll be home tomorrow morning to take care of everything."
"Okay Richard, it was great talking to you.
Just remember if there is anything I can do, please don't hesitate to give me a call. Goodbye."

It was 6am when Richard glanced at his watch as his flight began to descend into the airport at Fort Collins. "Right on time," he quietly murmured to himself. Richard's intentions were to surprise Veronica and the kids because they were not aware that he would be coming home today.

After acquiring his duffle bag from baggage claims, he made his way upstairs to hail a cab. He considered himself lucky because there was only a ten-minute wait before the cab arrived. "Where to soldier?" the cab driver asked with a hoarse tone.

After giving the driver the address, Richard was whisked off to his house. Within forty-five minutes, he was standing at his front door. "Now where did I put that key?" Richard began to search his coat pockets, and his pant pockets. Then suddenly, the door opened.

"Daddy!" Richard's daughter, Lesley, screamed with exhilaration as she ran into his arm, then she began to sob emotionally. "Daddy, you're home, I missed you so much!"

"There, there baby its okay." When Richard entered inside the house, he stepped into chaos and he was shocked by the frightening appearance of his house. He grasped for words to describe the deplorable conditions inside. "Wow! What is going on in here?" Clothes, shoes, and toys, were scattered all over the floor. Dishes were overflowing out the sink, and the house reeked of urine. "Veronica!" Richard yelled with fury. "Lesley where is Veronica?"

"Daddy she's asleep. She sleeps all the time."

As Richard walked down the hall to the bedroom, the other children emerged from their bedrooms. "Daddy, you're home!" their screams were filled with joyfulness.

Richard paused for a moment to hug and kiss his children, and then proceeded to Veronica's bedroom. When he opened the bedroom door, once again he was stunned by the shocking conditions within the room. "Veronica!" He discovered Veronica lying beneath a stack of blankets and clothes. He began throwing these items to the floor, grabbing Veronica, gingerly shaking her.

"Veronica, what's going on? First of all, you're in here laid out and Lesley opened the door! Now what if I would have been a rapist or burglar? Then you and all the children would have been in danger!"

Gazing through tired, weary eyes, Veronica finally snapped to herself. "Richard...baby you're home!" A sigh of relief was heard in Veronica's voice as tears began streaming down her face. With a slow unsteady movement, and with the assistance of Richard's strong arm, Veronica placed her feet on the floor. Then she stood up and embraced Richard around his waist.

"Veronica, are you all right?"

"Yes, I'm okay, but I'm just so tired all the time."

"Veronica, look around you, when was the last time you cleaned this room? I walked into the house and I saw stuff lying everywhere, the dishes are stacked in the sink, and the house smells like urine! What is going on?"

Speaking in an unapologetic tone, Veronica took this opportunity to express her emotions. "As I said, I'm so tired. I mean, I work all the time I have taken care of the children for six months alone. I try to keep this house clean, but it doesn't do any good because the kids always mess it up! Richard, now that you're home, maybe you could pitch in and help me!" Without saying anything else, Veronica quickly turned, walked into the bathroom, and locked the door.

Veronica's actions infuriated Richard so he went to the door and began knocking, demonstrating signs of fury, and he demanded Veronica to open the door. "Veronica open this door!" There was no response.

Now all the children were in the bedroom huddled together, expressing signs of fear that was brought on by the disturbance of their parents. "Daddy STOP!" Lesley's scream provoked the other children to cry. Richard did as his daughter demanded and ceased from knocking on the door. "Kids I'm so sorry, daddy didn't mean to frighten you. Come here." Motioning to the children, they timidly walked in his direction and he placed his arms around them.

It was then that Veronica emerged from the bathroom and noticed what was taking place.

"Kids could you wait for mommy and daddy in the other room, I need to speak to your mom for a minute." With a quick rush, the children left the room. Veronica appeared to be somewhat bewildered and was not sure what to expect from Richard. Both sat on the side of the bed and for a brief moment, neither spoke a word.

"Veronica, I want a divorce." Richard's words were cold and callous and nothing could have prepared Veronica for this untimely news. "I don't love you anymore. When I was in Savannah, I went back and forth about my decision but after coming back home to this pigpen, it has really helped me come to this conclusion. I mean, look at you! You look like hell! My stomach turns when I look at you!" It was as if a demon had possessed Richard's mind.

Stunned by his statement and with a blank stare, Veronica's tear stained eyes met those of Richard's. For a brief moment, Veronica said nothing. She was in shock and struggled to find the words to express the torment she was experiencing. Finally, she managed to utter two words. "A divorce?" she spoke with a slow murmur. "But what about the children? How can you just walk off and abandon the children?" she asked in a hushed tone.

Slowly Richard stood up and walked to the door. Sluggishly reaching for the doorknob he opened the door and started walking out but decided to answer Veronica's question. "For now, I'll leave Lesley and Selena here until I make arrangements with my parents to take care of them, and when I get settled somewhere, they will come live with me.

I'll talk to the kids and try to explain what my plans are. I'll return tomorrow and pack a few things." With those final words, Richard left the house.

Veronica continued to sit motionless in shocked from her encounter with Richard. She was in utter disbelief of what had just taken place. She found herself too weak to argue or to fight for her marriage. What good would it do anyway, because she knew Richard's demeanor. Once he had his mind made up to do something, there was no way he would change his mind.

Hurt both physically and mentally and lacking the strength to move off the bed, Veronica made the decision to crawl back into bed and cover herself with the bundle of blankets where Richard found her. There she remained the entire night. The next morning, she was awakened when she heard the front door slam. Peering out the window and slyly opening the side of the curtain she peered out and watched Richard ride away in a taxi. Apparently, he came to the house early that morning and packed his clothes.

Tears immediately began flowing down her face and in a small quiet voice she whispered, "Richard, what goes around, will come around."

CHAPTER 31

Youngstown, Ohio

Richard rented a car at the airport to make the trip to his parent's home. At 8am he pulled into the driveway, parked the car, and sat for a few moments taking in the view of the small framed house. In Richard's opinion, the house was falling apart and was in dire need of repairs. The white paint was chipping off the entire house, the front porch had almost caved in, and several other unsightly mishaps grasped Richard's attention.

He was sixteen years old when he left his hometown of Youngstown Ohio. The eldest of five siblings, it was his mother's wish that Richard leave his home to attend a well-known Seventh Day Adventist school in Pennsylvania. For many years, she tediously worked as a maid to save the money needed for her son's education.

Richard's mother completed high school, but she was determined that her children had the opportunity to excel and become whatever they wanted to be so she always inspired Richard and his siblings to continue their education.

Education was the main objective as to why Richard's mother wanted him to leave home. The second objective was even more crucial it was because of the horrible relationship that Richard had with his father, which was in a sense even more pressing. Among all the children, it appeared that Richards' father was at odds with him on a constant basis and getting him away from his father was an inevitable must.

Richard never understood the reason for the conflict between him and his father. However, his mother had a suspicion that perhaps it was the reflection of himself that was seen when he gazed into the face of his eldest son. Perhaps it was a reflection that reminded him of his own morbid past that he could not forget. Whatever the case, Richard's mother knew if her son was going to escape the tormented life that he was experiencing he had to leave Youngstown, Ohio.

Now sixteen years later, Richard was about to come face to face with his father. He had called and spoken with his mother the night before to explain the reason for his visit. He had hoped that she had shared the news with his father because it was not his desire to engage in a lengthy conversation with his dad if he could avoid doing so.

Engulfed in his thoughts, Richard was unaware that his father was standing behind his car until he heard a loud slam on the trunk of the car. With a quick jerk, Richard peered into his rear-view mirror to see what was going on, and that's when he saw his father standing by the trunk of his car. "Sergeant McWilliams, open your trunk so I can get your bags out." Roger McWilliams stated in a stern tone. Roger McWilliams had been a sergeant in the Korean War. "You do have bags in your trunk, don't you?"

Richard got out of the car and went around, joining his father at the back. His father glared at Richard up and down like a search light. "How are you, dad?"

"All right I suppose." Roger muttered with a condescending tone. "Did you bring any luggage, or did you just pack an overnight bag?" he asked trying to express humor.

"An overnight bag, I'm here to discuss some business with you and mama, and then I have to return to Fort Collins."

"Well come on inside. Your mama has prepared dinner for you, and after dinner, we can sit down and discuss how we can help you out."

Richard was shocked by the affable greeting he'd just received from his dad. What had happened to his father? Perhaps it was true that time does bring about a change? The actions of his father proved to be a perfect example of this statement. Once inside the house, Richard was affectionately greeted by his mother who was overtaken by the sight of her son and it brought her to tears. "Look at you!" she shouted with joy. "I am so glad to see you! It has been so long since I laid eyes on my baby boy!" Richard's mother grabbed him around his neck, and he collapsed into her arms, displaying his desperate need for affection and embracement of love.

"Mama, I'm so glad to see you, I have missed you so much." Richard could not contain the emotions he was experiencing at that moment and he began weeping uncontrollably. It was as if all the heartache and all the pain he had endured over the years were overtaking his soul. The comfort of his mother's loving arms was now the consoling medicine that was needed to soothe his broken heart and spirit.

"Okay son, let's sit down and eat, then we can talk about how we can help you out." Richard's father had walked away for a moment to allow his wife to have a tender moment with Richard.

"No Roger, let him go wash up and I'll have his plate ready when he returns." Richard's mother spoke in a compassionate voice.

After dinner, Richard informed his parents that he had asked Veronica for a divorce and he asked his parents would it be possible for them to take care of Lesley and Selena for a few months until he was settled into his own place.

Richard's parent were somewhat puzzled by his decision to divorce Veronica based on the reasons that he had given. "Richard I don't understand your decision for getting a divorce." His mother voiced her opinion. "Veronica has all those kids to take care of, and she works full time at the hospital. So, you're telling your father and me that you're divorcing her because she doesn't keep the house clean? You can't be serious!"

Frustration clouded Richard's mind because it appeared that his appeal concerning Veronica was not going very well with his parents. In fact, his parent had suggested that he would be making a terrible mistake if he left his wife.

"Richard, it's not about you, and I have to be truthful with you son, you're being selfish. Have you taken into consideration the hardships your wife is going through? What about the children? Have you considered the hardship this is going to bring on them?" Richard's mother asked harshly.

"Son, we both think this is a bad decision and no real man would walk off and leave a good wife like Veronica and his children! How will she provide for those kids? Son, if you do this I don't believe God will be pleased with your decision, and my biggest fear is that one day your decision will come back to haunt you. I suggest you go home, and try to work things out with your wife. As I told you before you married Veronica, you should have just concentrated on raising your children and left those women alone." "Yes, this is what I meant when I said you should marry your children I guess I should have explained myself better." Richard's father aimlessly tried to get his point across to his son. However, this was not the answer Richard had expected from his parents and it was obvious that they were not in agreement with his decision to divorce Veronica.

Richard sat down to compose himself because a sudden feeling of defeat was beginning to overtake him and he felt himself losing his balance. "So you're not going to help me out by taking Lesley and Selena?" he asked dryly.

"Richard, go home, sit down with your wife, and work this out." Richard's father was convinced that the marriage could be saved but Richard had made up his mind to divorce Veronica. If his parents were not going to help him with his children, he would somehow manage himself.

Rising from his seat, Richard thanked his parents for dinner and for taking time out to listen to his dilemma. He hugged his mother good bye, shook his father's hand, and was about to walk out the door but suddenly changed his mind. Turning back, he asked his father's permission to go into the basement. When this question was asked, both parents glared at each other in confusion. His father inquired. "The basement? Richard, it's been over sixteen years since you've been in this house, so what could be in the basement that you want to see?" He inquired with curiosity.

"Unresolved issues?" Richard replied expressing bitterness as he stared into the face of his father. "That basement holds skeletons I need to unleash before I leave here."

"Skeletons?" His father repeated with a whisper. Richard's father could not look him in the eyes, because he knew exactly what his son meant. Motioning in the direction of the basement, Richard walked slowly out of sight of his parents.

When he approached the door, he froze in his footsteps and reflected on the past grief he had suffered as a child in that basement. Did he really want to open that dreadful wound? Yes, he had to put closure to his skeletons so he could move on.

Slowly, his sweaty hands reached for the doorknob as he slowly began opening the door.

Once inside, visions of the past swiftly ran through his mind and a spirit of sadness overtook Richard. He became overwhelmed and sat down on the steps leading downward into the basement.

Sitting there for a moment to compose himself, Richard reflected on all the tragedies he had experienced since leaving this horrible place. However, when he began reflecting on the most dreadful tragedy of all, which was the death of his beautiful wife Carol, he knew that if he had survived her death surely he could face the past horrors in that basement.

Richard stood up and continued walking down the steps and his eyes fixated on one particular area where he had suffered the physical and mental abuse from his father. His heart ached with pain and his eyes welled with tears as he reflected on the cruel actions he had endured. Whenever his father would punish Richard, he used a technique that would have landed him in prison if it were ever reported to the authorities. His father would hang him by his feet with his head dangling downward and beat him with a large belt. These boisterous behaviors of Richard's father caused him to hate his father for many years. There was also the conundrum between him and his mother as well because she did nothing to stop this abnormal behavior of his father.

Richard stood in silence for a moment taking in deep breaths and exhaling them with a sigh of surrender as he continued to reflect on the grace and mercy of survival.

Yes, he had suffered the hideous beatings of his father, but he had survived. Yes, he was drafted into the army, and went to Vietnam, but he had survived.

Yes he had lost the love of his life, but he had survived.

At that moment, Richard was overtaken by a sense of peace, his heart was filled with gratitude, and in a whisper he murmured, "Daddy I forgive you." Tears began soaking his face, and he knelt and wept for what seemed like an hour. When he had emptied himself from all his past impurities, he got up and walked out of the basement, leaving behind the skeletons that had tormented him for years.

He made a pact with himself that he would never open old wounds from his past.

CHAPTER 32

Richard left his parents house with a sense of directions for his future. , He returned to Fort Collins and filed for divorce from Veronica. He took his two daughters, Lesley and Selena, returned to Savannah, and resumed his position as a trainer.

Six months later, while gazing out the window at his office, Richard saw this beautiful woman walk by. Immediately stopping his duties, he rushed outside to get a better glimpse of this woman. However, it was too late and the woman was nowhere in sight.

Returning to his office, Richard made an announcement to his co-workers. "Gentlemen, I must warn you that the beautiful woman your eyes have just seen will someday be my wife. Therefore if you guys just happen to bump into her anywhere, don't try to talk to her because I've already claimed her. So if you all will excuse me I am going back outside to search for my new wife."

Richard spent his entire lunch break looking for this mystery woman but without success. Thirty minutes later, he returned to the office with an expression of defeat. "Sergeant, did you find your mystery wife?" his co-workers in the office playfully inquired.

"No, but if it's meant to be, I will see her again." Richard spoke with confidence.

Richard was accurate in his assumption because three hours later, this same woman walked past his office. Richard didn't see her walk by, but his co-worker, Stanley, noticed her graciously walking past his office. "Sergeant, I just saw your mystery woman walk by."

With an excited gesture, Richard quickly ran out the office looking for this woman. Finally, he saw her and with the speed of a super hero, he ran in her direction and began yelling, "Excuse me, ma'am!" The woman continued walking because she was unaware that he was trying to get her attention. So, Richard screamed louder when he saw her getting into her car. "Excuse me, ma'am!"

Then it happened. Slowly she turned and faced Richard, and her eyes fixated on his and Richard's heart skipped a thousand beats because he was overwhelmed by the physical appearance of this woman and he found himself speechless for a brief moment. However, he knew he had to say something, or he would miss this opportunity. "Ma'am, I'm sorry I didn't mean to yell at you, but I was only trying to get your attention."

"Okay, you have my attention, now what do you want because I have some place to be in about ten minutes," she replied with a sharp quick tone.

Richard extended his hand to the woman with the attention of shaking her hand but his actions were not receptive. "I'm Richard McWilliams and I just wanted to see if I could give you my phone number and…"

"Sir, right now, I really don't have time to stand here and listen to you trying to hit on me. Thanks, but no thanks because I am not interested in you or any man at the moment. So if you would excuse me." With those last words, the mystery woman opened the door to her car and placed the key in the ignition.

Richard knew he had to do something he couldn't just let her drive off without knowing her name or getting her phone number. "Ma'am please could I give you my business card? Please Ma'am!" he pleaded.

The woman took his card, and drove off. Richard was not sure if he would ever see this woman again, but it was definitely his heart's desire to do so.

He walked slowly back to his office trying to decide on a convincing fabrication to tell his co-workers. Surely he couldn't tell them he had been ditched by this gorgeous woman, because he would surely look like a fool in front of everyone. The moment Richard arrived in the office, his co-worker Stanley rushed over to tell Richard that he had an emergency phone call from his mother. Quickly he rushed over to his desk and called his mother. "Hello? Mom what's wrong?" His voice was filled with anxiety.

"Richard, it's your father. He passed away a few hours ago." His mother replied, whimpering through each spoken word.

"Mom what happened?" Richard inquired expressing concern for his mother. Yes, Richard was sadden about the death of his father, but hearing the desperate tone in his mother's voice shook him to the core. Richard's mother was his first love and his relationship with his mother superseded the relationship he had with his father.

"Richard, the doctors are not sure, what happened to him and they won't know until they do an autopsy. Son, I need you to come home to help me through this crisis. Richard, could you please come home?" his mother asked with a desperate plea.

"Yes ma'am, I'll get there as soon as possible."

"Thank you Richard, I'll see you soon, son."

Richard was in disbelief by the sudden death of his father.

"What's going on, Sergeant?" Stanley inquired.

"My dad just passed away, and I'm going back home to help my mom take care of the funeral arrangements."

"Sergeant, we're sorry to hear that." His co-workers replied, expressing sympathy.

"If you all will excuse me, let me get on the horn and make a call to Colonel Ruddick so I can request some time off." Richard had no idea how much time he would need in order to take care of his business back home. Perhaps two weeks would do it. He also knew that he would have to take the girls with him as well. Therefore, he had to make arrangements to take them out of school for two weeks.

When everything was arranged later on that evening, Richard and the girls were on their way to Ohio. As he drove in solitude, his mind drifted back to a familiar moment in time when he was driving with his children in the back seat of his Volkswagen. That was when his sweet wife Carol lost her life in the accident.

Although it had been ten years since that tragic day, the memory still lingered freshly in his mind and perhaps, it would always remain with him for the rest of his life.

CHAPTER 33

The day of the funeral arrived and the small church on Galloway Street overflowed with people paying their last respects to Richard's father. He was puzzled as to how a cruel, brutal man such as his father could have so many people show up for his funeral. Perhaps over the years his father had transformed into an upstanding man of God, rather than the child abusive tyrant that Richard had known.

With inquisitiveness, Richard watched the face of each person that passed by the blue and white casket that held the remains of his father. Each person would stop for a brief moment to take their last gaze upon his father's face. Then they would turn to Richard's mother and his siblings, who were all seated on the front row to express words of sympathy. This made Richard very uncomfortable and he would be extremely thankful when the funeral was over.

One hour, and forty-five minutes later, Richard and his family left the church and went through the last phase of the ceremony at the cemetery. The body of his father was lowered into the grave and after everyone had left, Richard chose to remain alone by the gravesite. "So this is it," he murmured. "I didn't have a chance to tell you face to face, but daddy I forgive you. I will never understand why you were so mean to me, but I forgive you." Tears were streaming down Richard's face and he felt his knees begin to weaken, failing to hold up his six foot four frame.

Suddenly he felt a slight tug on his coat and he heard a voice that snapped him back into reality. "Daddy, are you okay?" Slowly Richard turned and peered into the sweet face of his daughter Lesley. "Daddy, are you okay?" Lesley repeated with concern.

"Yes sweetheart, daddy's okay, I'm just saying my final goodbyes to your grandpa. Come on let's go find your grandma and your sister." He took the hand of his daughter and walked away, closing that chapter of his life.

Richard and his daughters spent the next few days with his mother, helping her sort out bills, and doing some much needed chores around the house. After a week, he decided it was time to return to Savannah and spend the last few days of his leave of absence working at his own house.

When he returned to work, he had a nice surprise waiting for him. On his desk was a beautiful flower arrangement along with a card. "Didn't you guys already send flowers for my dad's funeral?" he asked.

"We sure did." Stanley replied with a hint of humor.

"So, who sent these flowers?" Richard inquired with curiosity.

"Sir, just read the card," everyone replied.

With excitement, Richard quickly ripped open the envelope and began reading the card. Everyone watched closely and noticed an expression of exhilaration appear in Richard's eyes. Suddenly, Richard yelled with excitement. "She sent the flowers!"

"She who?" Everyone asked.

In a long breath, Richard replied. "The woman I saw a few weeks ago. You know, the woman that passed by the office that I went chasing after.

"Oh yeah, the mystery woman, now we remember. So what's her name, did she put her name and phone number on the card?" Stanley asked.

"Stanley, that's my business, don't you think?" Richard replied with sarcasm. Then with a big, grin he replied. "Just kidding, yep I got both a phone number, and a name!" Peering inside the card, he read the name. "Ellen Frasier. So how did she know that my father passed away?" Richard asked with a curious tone.

"Sir, she came by two days after you left for Ohio and said you had given her a business card but she had misplaced the card. She came by the office to see you and we told her that your father had passed away and you went to Ohio for the funeral," Stanley replied.

Whatever the case, Richard was pleased with the fact that Ellen Frasier had shown interest in him. It was the spark of happiness that he needed to uplift his spirits.

CHAPTER 34

"Hello could I speak to, Ellen?" Nervousness could be heard in Richard's voice.

"Yes this is Ellen. Who's calling?"

"This is Sergeant Richard McWilliams, and I'm calling to thank you for the beautiful flowers you sent to my office for my father.

"Sergeant McWilliams, you are quite welcome. It was my pleasure, and I am so sorry to hear about the passing of your father. Let me personally offer you my condolences. I lost my father last year, so I can relate to the pain you're feeling right now." Ellen's voice was soothing to Richard's ears.

"Thank you Ellen. I really appreciate your kindness. Now how can I show my appreciation? What if I took you out to dinner? You can choose the restaurant, just tell me when and where, and I'll be there."

"Thanks Richard, that is not necessary but if you insist, let's make plans to go to Atlanta and hang out there I'm sure we can find something fun to do in Atlanta."

"Okay, that sounds great! But I have to inform you up front, I'm a single father, I have two daughters, Lesley is eight and Selena is six so, I have to plan ahead and make arrangement for a baby sitter if we're going to Atlanta."

"I understand because I'm a single parent also. I have a son, he's eight, and his name is Jackson."

"That's great!" Richard remarked with excitement. "Finally I've met a woman who can relate to what's it like being a single parent."

"Yes, it's only been me and Jackson for the past two years. His dad died in a tragic car accident so with work and taking care of my little man, I don't have time for much of anything else."

"I understand, because my girls keep me busy as well." With hesitation, Richard continued his conversation. "Ellen, I don't want to seem forward but maybe when you have time we could get together and take the kids to the park, or to the zoo."

"Sure, that sounds like fun. Jackson is always ready to go somewhere, but I am more of a homebody. I go to work, come home and that's it."

"Well, my girls and I are going to get you and Jackson out of that boring life style and put a little action into your lives. You just let me know when you can fit us into your busy schedule," Richard replied with a sense of happiness.

"Oh I will definitely let you know," Ellen replied.

"Once again, thank you so much for the flowers and I hope I'll get the opportunity to talk with you real soon. We'll work on that trip to Atlanta, in the near future. I'll talk to you real soon."

Richard hung up the phone and felt a renewed sense of happiness and excitement. There was something special about this woman that attributed to the emotions he was feeling. He couldn't quite determine what, but if time permitted, he was going to find out why he was so turned on by Miss Ellen Frasier.

The days that followed did reveal that *special thing* that made Richard feel all warm and toasty in side. He, Ellen, and the children were always together. He was the father that Ellen's son never had and Ellen was an exemplary image of a mother for Richard's daughters.

Richard took Ellen and her son to Ohio to meet his mother and she was very impressed with Ellen. Therefore, with the approval of his mother, once again Richard remarried. Ellen would be wife number six and Richard vowed to himself that if this marriage did not work out, he would never marry again.

CHAPTER 35

Five Years Later

"Ellen!" Richard was frantically searching throughout the house looking for his wife, to tell her about the new job offer he had just received. "Ellen, where are you?"

Rushing inside from the backyard, Ellen approached Richard breathless. "Richard what's wrong? Did something happen?" she asked in a hysterical tone.

Handing her a business card, Richard began to speak with excitement. "Baby this little card is going to be a blessing to us," he stated with excitement.

"Richard, I don't understand what you mean," Ellen replied with a confused expression.

"Okay let me back up and start from the beginning. On my way home, I stopped by the record store on Lake Drive and I was walking around looking at some gospel music and this guy, named Jack Harley, came up to me and asked if I liked gospel music. I told him yes, and then he said he owned several radio stations all over the country and he needed someone to come to his station downtown to play gospel music. He said he was in town for a few days because he needed to hire a DJ for his station. He asked if I would be interested in coming to his radio station to try out for the job.

Ellen you know me, I'm always up for a challenge, so I told him I would come by the station. I went to the radio station, played a few records, and baby, I love it!"

Ellen was not sure if she wanted to hear what Richard was going to say next. Surely he wasn't considering quitting the military to become a radio DJ. She just had to ask the question. "Richard, are you telling me you're considering leaving the military to become a radio DJ?" Ellen was frustrated.

"Yes, that's what I'm saying. Truthfully, I'm burned out with the military and I am ready for a change. My contract will be over in three months and I am not considering re-enlisting. I told Mr. Harley after work I would come to the radio station and work at night for him. This way I will be able to get a little more experience under my belt. When I get the hang of things, and if I enjoy what I'm doing, then I will accept his offer as a full time employee."

At this point, Ellen had lost her patience listening to Richard's ridiculous decision to become a radio DJ. "Well Richard, it appears that you have already made your decision."

"Yes I have. Baby don't worry everything is going to be fine. What's the problem?"

Anger elevated in Ellen's voice. "The problem is I cannot believe that you would just throw away all the years you've served in the military for some wild idea of becoming a DJ! I just don't understand!"

Richard took Ellen's hands and gently squeezed them. Gazing into her sweet face, he tried to find words to comfort her heart. "Sweetheart, I don't quite know how to explain this, but when I went to that radio station and started playing that music, I felt as if that was what I was born to do. Playing those records made me feel alive and excited and I had a sense of fulfillment. Working as a recruiter and a trainer for the army…it doesn't make me feel fulfilled or happy. That's how I know it is time for me to change careers. So could you just be happy for me? It's going to be fine. When I meet with Mr. Harley I'll make sure I negotiate a salary that will provide for my family, ok?" Richard spoke with confidence.

Ellen knew after being married to this man for nearly five years, she could trust him and have confidence in his decisions. He had been a wonderful father and an excellent provider, so she knew he would never put the wellbeing of his family in jeopardy. "Okay Richard, I'm in your corner, we'll see how this radio DJ career turns out," Ellen replied with contentment.

A glow of satisfaction came over Richard's face once he knew Ellen was in his corner he could move forward.

Three months later, when Richard's contract ended with the military, he took the full time position at the radio station. A year later, his decision paid off. He was promoted to a general manager's position at a radio station in New Orleans. Richard and his family packed up and left Savannah.

In New Orleans, Richard's new career exceeded his expectations and he excelled to new heights. Soon he was the general manager over two other radio stations. One station was located in Washington, and the other one in Houston. This, however, meant that Richard would have to travel on numerous occasions to these stations each month.

Although his residence was in New Orleans, his only regret was the fact that he would have to leave his family in order to travel to these other places. While Richard was excelling in his career and was acknowledged as one of the paramount general managers in the radio industry, his family was suffering due to his absence. His wife was overwhelmed with the responsibility of taking care of the children, and their home. In addition, living in the shadows of Richard's sudden popularity was taking a toll on Ellen.

When Richard was approached by his wife with her concerns, she was not pleased with the outcome. "Richard, I know your work is demanding, but is there any way you could ask for a little time off? Maybe two weeks so you and I and the kids could take a short vacation somewhere together?" Ellen asked with a plea in her voice.

Richard had just returned home from a trip to Houston, and had only spent two days at home and now he was packing a suitcase preparing for a trip to Washington. "Ellen, I'm sorry, I've got too much to do, and a vacation is completely out of the question. Honey, you're going to have to suck it up, because traveling comes with the territory. And let me also remind you how fortunate you are that you're married to a man that works his butt off providing for you. Ellen, look around… you live in a beautiful house, you drive a nice car, I pay all the bills, and you haven't worked a day since we've been married.

Trust me there are plenty of women who would gladly trade places with you any day. So what are you complaining about?" Richard spoke with arrogance. Yes, his popularity had definitely gone to his head and he began displaying a mean, selfish attitude towards his wife, his staff, and friends. He was out of control it was as if his mind had been taken over by a prideful demon spirit.

Whenever he was at home, there was friction among him, his wife, and the kids. He would scream and yell at everyone as if he was an out of control tyrant. Everything had to be his way or no way. The pressure was too much for Ellen, she began having severe headaches due to the pressure and stress she was going through, and she required constant medical attention.

Richard's daughters and Ellen's son, Jackson, were also extremely unhappy living in these unbearable conditions. Richard's daughters were extremely fearful of their father whenever he went on his unpredictable rampages by screaming and yelling at them for every little thing they did.

Richard was not aware that his daughters had contacted his mother and had pleaded with her to take them in. When Richard heard about his daughters' plans, he was outraged. In anger, he made the hasty decision to allow his daughters live with his mother but in the end, his decision would prove to be a disaster for him.

CHAPTER 36

New Orleans, 5 years later

It was getting late and Ellen had not heard from Richard all day. This was quite unusual because throughout the day, on most occasions, he would call at least twice to see how her day was going and to check on Jackson. However today, for some odd reason, he had broken his routine and Ellen was getting worried. Then the phone rang.

"You're where?" Ellen screamed in a hysterical tone.

"Ellen don't worry, everything is going to be okay, I just had a little misunderstanding with one of my clients, and he called the police, so they brought me downtown. Stupid me, I lost my temper and said something I shouldn't have, and they threw me in jail," Richard said with a sorrowful tone.

Ellen was bewildered and stunned by what had happened to her husband and her level of anxiety escalated to its highest height. "Richard, what do you want me to do?" she muttered and fear was heard in her voice.

"Nothing, I have a friend who's on his way down here to bail me out. I just wanted you to know what happened before you saw it on television or heard about it on the radio. Baby, don't worry everything will be fine. I'll see you later on tonight. I love you Ellen and I'm so sorry I put you through all this drama." Richard abruptly hung up the phone.

Ellen placed the phone on the receiver and minutes after, Jackson entered the room.

With excitement, Jackson inquired, "Mom was that pops on the phone?" Jackson adored Richard he was the only father figure he'd known his entire life. Ellen's heart was breaking after receiving this heart-wrenching phone call from Richard. Ellen didn't know what to say to Jackson because she didn't want him to worry.

Trying to conceal any outward emotional expression of sadness, Ellen tried to pull herself together before replying to her son. "Yes Jackson, that was your pops, he's working late, and he said

not to wait up for him tonight because you'd probably be asleep when he gets home."

"No, I'll wait up for him because I need his help with my math. He said he would help me yesterday and since you're not good in math, mom, you know pops will have to help me."

"Okay, Jackson, if Richard makes it home in time, I'll send him to your room so he can help you. If he doesn't make it home on time, I'll write your teacher a note to inform her that your mother is too dumb to help her son with his math and your pops was too tired," Ellen replied with humor.

This brought a smile to Jackson's handsome face. "Mom, you ain't dumb, pop's just smart in math!"

"Okay thank you, and there is no such word as, *ain't*. It is *not*. Now go to bed."

Since the death of his father, Jackson had always been Ellen's ray of sunshine. Whenever the chips were down, she could always focus her attention on her son, and life always was brighter.

It was 1:00am in the morning when Richard finally made it home. The moment he arrived, he quietly went into Jackson's room, got his math book, and took it into the bedroom where Ellen was anxiously waiting. The moment Richard opened the door, Ellen quickly rushed into his arms. "Richard, are you okay?" she asked with concern.

"Yes, I'm fine. As I told you on the phone, I had a little misunderstanding with one of my clients. I got frustrated and I lost my temper, he lost his temper and one thing lead to another. When I told him to get out of my office he refused, so, I grabbed him and escorted him out the door. That's when he called the police and he told them that I assaulted him.

The police took me downtown, but they never went through the process of booking me because my client reconsidered and came to the police station to drop the charges. He apologized for his actions, so they let me go and my friend didn't have to bail me out after all. Now, before I go to bed, I'm going to help Jackson with his math problems like I promised."

"You're going to wake him up?" Ellen asked.

"Yes, I'm going to wake him up. I promised I would help him and that's what I'm going to do."

"But Richard, it's after one o'clock in the morning."

"I know…what time did he go to bed?"

"Eight o'clock like all ways.

"He's been asleep for five hours. So I'll wake him up and it shouldn't take any more than an hour to work these problems. Then he can go back to bed and he can sleep until seven thirty and I'll drop him off at school tomorrow." With those last words, Richard left the room.

Relieved that Richard made it home safely and confident that her son was going to get assistance with his math, Ellen snuggled under the covers in her bed and with an immediate smile of gratification, she quickly fell asleep. Regardless of the turbulence that had occurred earlier that day, in the end, it still turned out to be a good day after all.

CHAPTER 37

"Dallas?" Richard shouted with surprise. Three days later after the heated altercation with his client, Richard was summoned to the office of his boss, Mr. Harley.

"Richard, the board members and I held a meeting this morning and we have decided that because of the publicity that was brought on concerning your run in with your client, for the best interest of the company, we have decided to have you relocate to our branch office in Dallas."

"C'mon Mr. Harley, you can't be serious! I have apologized to the client and I have apologized to you and the board. What else do I have to do?"

Richard inquired with anguish.

"Richard, I'm really sorry. I realize you are a valuable asset to the company and I really hate to lose you. However, my hands are tied because I take my orders from the board of directors and their decision is final. Look at it this way, you are still working for the company, but you will just be in another state. Hell, in my opinion, I think you will do great things in Dallas."

Richard sat and stared for a moment into the face of his boss before asking his question. "Why would you think that I would do great things in Dallas?"

"Richard, Dallas is a wide open market for gospel radio. There is only one gospel radio station there, and I think it is in need of some competition.

With your experience and perseverance, I personally believe you're the right man to give them a run for their money.

So, don't look at this as being a setback because you have to leave New Orleans. Look at it as being a great opportunity that in the end will be a blessing to you and your family. A few days ago, I sent my son, Roger, to Dallas and he's located the office, set it up, and hired three people to get things started. However, what the station needs is the right person to build it up and really get it going. As I said in the beginning of our conversation, Richard, you are that person. I suggest that you take advantage of this opportunity and make the best out of it. Are you up for the challenge?"

After the conversation with Mr. Harley, Richard was beginning to get a new perspective about moving to Dallas. Perhaps this would be the perfect opportunity for him and his family to get back on track. After all, since moving to New Orleans, he had been under a ton of stress from working long hours and the pressure of traveling and being away from his family had brought about the breakdown of his relationship with his daughters and with his wife.

Yes, perhaps starting over in Dallas would be a welcoming change for Richard. "Okay Mr. Harley, I'll go to Dallas. Maybe the change would be good for me and my family. Sir, let me ask you something, when I transfer to Dallas will there be a big demand for me to travel to DC and to Houston?"

"As a matter of fact, no, not as much as you're doing now. Since you will be living in Texas, I think we can get by on just letting you travel to Houston on a few occasions. Otherwise, you'll be able to stay in Dallas with your family. How does that sound?" Mr. Harley walked over, placed his hands on Richard's shoulder and smiled, waiting for an indication of appreciation from Richard.

Richard, you can take the rest of day off, go home, and talk to your family about your transfer. The board and I will pay your traveling expenses, and we've agreed to pay three months of rent for you and your family. This way you and Ellen can start looking for a place to live. Your last day here in the office will be thirty days from now. I tried to get you more time, but the board didn't agree to my request. Good luck to you, Richard. I'm flying back to Nashville tomorrow, but I'll be in Dallas in a few months to see how everything is going with you and your staff."

"Thank you Mr. Harley. I'm sure Ellen will be pleased with your generosity. That is once she gets over the initial shock of having to move to Dallas." Richard reached for Mr. Harley's hand, thanked him for his kindness, and walked out of the office.

When Richard arrived home, he paused for a moment and glanced at the small red brick home that he and Ellen had called home for the past five years. "Ellen loves this little house, and she has worked so tiresomely decorating and taking care of it. How am I going to explain to her that we have to move again? Lord please, make this easy for me." Richard was apprehensive about telling Ellen about the move to Dallas.

Richard's thoughts were interrupted when Jackson came rushing out the house. "Pops I saw your car drive up, me and mom have been waiting for you." Jackson was excited about something. He grabbed Richard's hand, and hurriedly pulled him inside the house.

Once inside, relief came when he saw Ellen wearing a cowboy hat. He was curious to find out what was going on.

Ellen flashed a big smile and said, "Baby, news travels fast."

With a look of confusion, Richard asked, "Ellen, what are you talking about?"

With exhilaration Ellen shouted, "Dallas! Aren't we moving to Dallas?"

"Who told you that we were moving to Dallas?" Richard asked.

Playfully Ellen replied, "A little birdie told me."

Once again, Richard asked the question, "Who told you?"

"Oh, I promised I wouldn't tell you who, but I can't lie to you sweetheart. Gail, the receptionist at your office called and said she overheard your conversation with Mr. Harley. So, is it true, are we moving to Dallas?"

Richard breathed a sigh of release. "Yes, it's true." Before he could continue, Ellen ran towards Richard, embracing him and planted a big, wet kiss on his lips. Richard was puzzled. "Wait, you mean you're excited about going to Dallas?"

"Oh yes, I'm ready to get out of this overcrowded, old run down, mosquito infested city. I cannot tell you how grateful I am to Mr. Harley that he's relocating you to Dallas. If he was standing here right now, I would give him a big kiss." After Ellen finished talking, she handed Richard a black cowboy hat. "Here you go, this is a little present Jackson and I bought for you. Go on, try it on."

Richard placed the hat on his head and with a satisfied sigh, he whispered, "Thank you Lord for answering my prayer. You made this easier than I could have ever imagined."

CHAPTER 38

Two years later

The transfer to Dallas would be the catalyst that would propel Richard into a successful career in the radio industry. His hard work and tenacious efforts paid off, and his radio station soared in sales and advertisements. The station was the number one gospel station in the state of Texas the first year he was the general manager.

Yes, things were looking up for Richard. He had acquired success, money, and fame but he never could escape the constant yearning for his children. Over the years, Richard's ex-wife, Veronica had remarried and her new husband refused to allow Richard to have any contact with his children. After numerous attempts, Veronica pleaded with Richard to give up his effort, because his actions only brought about chaos, and fiction between she and her husband.

Therefore, Richard had to make the sorrowful decision to abide by Veronica's wishes and give up his quest.

Richard began focusing his attention on Selena and Lesley. Since moving in with his mother, his daughters had spent several summer vacations with Richard, but his inevitable desire was to become more involved in their lives. He also was grateful that Rene and Harold allowed him to visit his son on numerous occasions, but he also wanted to request more time with him as well.

Yes, with urgency, Richard decided that getting things in order with his children was of the utmost importance. "Tomorrow," he murmured to himself and flashed a smile of satisfaction. "Next week I'm taking a few days off and I'm flying to Ohio to see my daughters." His thoughts were suddenly interrupted when the phone ranged. Glancing at the caller id, he noticed it was his mother's number. "Mom, I was just about to call you." His conversation ceased when he heard his mother crying on the phone. "Mom, what's wrong?" he inquired in a panic.

"Richard." His mother's voice staggered with agony. "Richard, Daniel is dead! His wife called and said they found his body at the bottom of a cliff!"

Richard could not believe what his mother was saying. "Mom, are you sure?" Richard didn't want to believe that his younger brother had died. Just the thought of his dying was like a knife cutting out his heart. Listening to his mother sobbing hysterically on the phone paralyzed his mind and it took a moment for him to continue the conversation. "Mom, what happened?" he managed to respond.

"Richard I don't know for sure, but please call your sister-in-law Cora. See if you can get more details." Her voice trembled with sorrow when she spoke.

"This really can't be happening." Richard murmured. Once again, Richard's life was about to be shattered from the darkness of death.

Richard's brother was a prominent pastor who had lived in Kingston, Jamaica for over ten years. He had a thriving ministry with over ten thousand members and was married to a native islander named Cora, whom he met in college. Richard began reflecting on the excitement of his brother when he started dating Cora. Richard was the first person Daniel called when he had made the decision to marry her, and he was the first person to know of his brother's plans to make Kingston his home.

Now at 39 years of age, his younger brother was dead. Once again, the sting of death was staring Richard directly in the face, and there was nothing he could do about it except grieve the loss of his brother.

A week later Richard and his family members flew to Kingston to attend his brother's funeral. The abundant attendance of people at the funeral demonstrated the popularity of Richard's brother. Well-wishers lined up to express their heartfelt sympathy for his brother but no words of expressions could console the broken void that was in the hearts of Richard and his family.

Not only was Richard and his family broken by the loss of Daniel, but there was no evidence as to how Daniel's lifeless body ended up at the bottom of a twenty foot cliff. There were never any suspects arrested and no clues to be found and as the years passed, Daniel's case eventually closed and the police called it an accident.

CHAPTER 39

Five years later

Richard had just come home from a business trip and found his wife gone, and his furniture gone, and his house empty. He called everyone who he thought would possibly know of her whereabouts including her best friend Cassie, her sister, and now his last resort, her mother. Just like the others, Ellen's mother also refused to give Richard any information concerning the whereabouts of his wife.

Walking outside his door, Richard noticed his neighbor Thomas sitting on the front porch. Richard knew his neighbor was aware of everything that went on in the neighborhood, so his last attempt was to see if Thomas had seen anything going on at his house. Reluctantly, Richard approached his neighbor.

"Thomas, I'm sorry to bother you, but I was wondering if you saw anything going on over at my house? I came back from my business trip and when I got home, my wife wasn't there, and my house is cleaned out," Richard stated and his eyes began to fill with tears.

Having compassion for Richard, Thomas invited him inside. "Richard, would you like to come inside or would you care for something to drink?" Thomas was an elderly retired man who very rarely had visitors, so having Richard in his mist was a welcoming occasion.

"No thank you Thomas, I just wanted to know if by chance you've seen my wife and my son?" Richard inquired with a sigh of anxiety.

With a slow long sigh, Thomas began to speak. "As a matter of fact I did see a big U-Haul truck pull up to your house about two days ago. I didn't think anything about it because I saw your wife and your boy help load some stuff on the truck. I just assumed that y'all were moving, but now since I see you standing here, I know that you weren't moving but your wife and son were. I'm sorry Richard but it appears that your wife has left you. Now, you sure I can't get you something to drink? Maybe a shot of whiskey?" Thomas replied showing both remorse and humor.

"Thank you Thomas, but I don't drink and thanks for the information." Feeling his control slipping, Richard bid goodbye to Thomas and returned to his house. Consumed with heartbreak, Richard fell onto the floor and began weeping like a child. "Why did she leave me? What did I do?" Richard yelled with agony.

Hidden within the deep contours of Richard's heart, he knew the truth, but he was in complete denial. Richard knew for the past two years that he had been unfaithful to his wife he had been involved in at least three affairs. However, what he didn't know was that his wife was aware of his actions.

Although Ellen had not given Richard the slightest indication that she knew what was going on, it was now obvious that she was fed up with his behavior and had decided to leave him.

A week passed and Richard was lost in a state of confusion and there was nothing he could do except to wait for Ellen to contact him. He had hoped with a little space between them, perhaps Ellen would have reached out to him by now.

However, two weeks passed, then a month passed and Ellen did not contact Richard. The second month after Ellen had moved, out he received a large envelope that contained a divorce decree. Richard was shocked! He didn't want a divorce. He had prayed that somehow he and Ellen could work things out, but after receiving his divorce decree, it was conclusive that the marriage was over. Richard's next step was to hire an attorney but he already had decided that he would not fight against any of Ellen's demand. He had hurt her enough because of his infidelities. His emotional guilt and baggage was killing him and the least he could do was to be civil and do the right thing. Yes, he was unfaithful to Ellen but he was still her husband and it was his responsibility to insure that Ellen had financial security. After all, his careless actions were the reason for the divorce anyway.

After the deliberations of the divorce were over, Richard noticed Ellen quickly making her way in his direction. When she approached him, she did not hesitate to ask Richard a question. Pain quivered in Ellen's voice. "Richard, why did you hurt me? What did I do wrong?" Tears began streaming down Ellen's face. "Why did you cheat on me Richard?" She was overtaken with anguish but continued to stare in his face and waited for a reply.

Richard was quiet for a moment and shame and condemnation came rushing over him like a blustering wind. Slowly, he turned his head and looked away, unable to withstand the glaring gaze in Ellen's tear stained eyes. At last, he spoke, but his answer was as unpredictable as the quandary that he had gotten himself into. "Ellen, I am so sorry I hurt you and if I could turn back the hands of time, I never would have made such a dreadful mistake." Richard's words were remorseful. "But the only excuse I can give you is... the devil made me do it."

Ellen's sister Nora was standing next to her, and when she heard Richard's unorthodox statement, in anger, she raised her hand to slap Richard's face. However, Ellen grabbed her sister by the arm and without another word, they quickly walked away. This would be the last time Richard would ever see Ellen.

Richard had a difficult time getting back into the swing of things, after his divorce, so he decided to take a long leave of absence to spend some quality time with his children and his mother.

The day Richard was preparing to return to Dallas, his mother gave him some much-needed words of encouragement. Gazing into Richard's eyes with motherly love and affection, Richard's mother spoke in a sweet quiet tone. "Son, don't give up you stay strong and hang in there, because God is not finished with you yet. Now, I know you have been married six times and to some people this might seem a little odd. However, the Bible does say that it is not good for a man to be alone. Richard, you still are a young man and if it is God's will, He will place your next wife in your pathway.

Richard, hear me well. If he does do this, be careful how you treat this woman, because as you know, number seven is God's perfect number. Do you understand what I am saying? Don't take her for granted because if you do, God will not be pleased with your actions." Richard's mother's words were serious and firm.

Richard did not appear to be receptive to his mother's advice because at that moment remarrying was the furthest thing from his mind. "Mom, right now, I don't have any desire to even look at a woman, not to mention marrying someone. I just want to concentrate on my career and take care of my children."

"I understand, but when that time comes, and it will come, after God heals your broken heart. I am just giving you some insight on what to do, because Richard if you blow it this time around, you will have to suffer the consequences. Just remember what I told you."

CHAPTER 40

After returning to Dallas, Richard threw himself into his work with a fearsome drive. He began traveling more often and he became active in the community. His radio station was a large promoter of education, school activities, and church activities.

One afternoon an individual, who happened to be a very talented musician, approached Richard about organizing a gospel choir. Since Richard had been a gifted choir director in his college days, he jumped at the opportunity to put together a choir. Immediately he began announcing on the radio station the need for choir members and within three days following his broadcast, he had over one hundred people willing and ready to join his choir.

After extensive auditions, Richard had narrowed the choir down to fifty singers and four musicians. The choir rehearsed extensively for over a month before Richard decided that "The Voices of Glory" choir was ready to perform. Richard's advantage was the fact that he was already acquainted with numerous churches in Dallas, Fort Worth, and the surrounding suburban areas because these churches broadcasted daily on his radio station.

When he approached the pastors to inquire about allowing his choir to perform at their churches, they considered it an honor to adhere to Richard's request.

Months of tiresome performances throughout Texas, and Richard's choir "The Voices of Glory" became a success. Everywhere the choir performed, people would pack the churches. They would receive standing ovations and praises for their angelic voices. To make the performances even sweeter, the pastors at each church always would collect a love offering to bless the choir, which many times would be a substantial amount of funds.

With the success of the choir, Richard's secretary Joyce became overwhelmed trying to maintain both her duties at the radio station and the duties of the choir. She suggested that Richard should hire someone as her personal assistant, and she did have some one in mind for the job.

"Richard, I know the perfect person for the job.

She is a friend of mine. I've known her for about five years. She's smart, well organized, attractive, and she can sing too. So not only would she be a great assistant, she could sing in the choir as well."

"Is she single?" Richard was suspicious.

"Yes."

"See…that's just what I thought, you're trying to set me up with this woman."

"No, that's not what I'm trying to do. I was trying to tell you that she's not married yet, but she's getting married in about three months."

"Oh, I'm sorry I thought you were trying to hook me up." Richard was embarrassed. "Yes, give her the address to the church, she can come by and I'll talk to her after rehearsal."

"Great, we'll see you then."

When Joyce and her friend arrived at the church, Richard was in deep concentration directing the choir. His arms were wildly waving to the beat of the music and his voice was extremely loud as he attentively tried to teach the tenor section their part to the song.

Gazing in Richard's direction with amazement, Joyce's friend asked a question. "Girl, who is that wild man up there?"

"That's Brother Richard he's the choir director, that's the guy you'll be talking to about the job."

"Are you serious? He looks like a mad man! Look at the gleam in his eyes, and my goodness, he is so loud! I've never seen anyone like him in my life!"

"I know right? I have to agree with you, he is a little odd, but I can vouch for him because I have known him for three years, and I can truthfully say that he is a real nice person and you will have a blast working with him. He's funny, he's flamboyant, he's a go getter, and he loves spending money. Trust me, he has taken us to places we never thought we would we go," Joyce remarked with excitement.

"Okay, well, I'm here now so, I'll check things out and if it's something I want to become a part of, then so be it."

"Trust me you are going to love your new job.

Look here comes Brother Richard. Brother Richard, this is the young lady I was telling you about. This is Ms. Rachel Tatum."

"Nice to meet you Rachel. I'm Richard McWilliams, but everybody calls me Brother Richard. Joyce has told me so much about you. Has she explained what you'll being doing for the choir?"

"Yes sir, I'll assist Joyce with whatever she wants me to do."

"Ok, now that's what I call getting straight to the point."

"Brother Richard, when do I start?"

"So, if that's a yes, Joyce will fill you in on all the details. It was nice to meet you Rachel but I have one more song to direct so I hope to see you soon."

"Thank you Brother Richard for this opportunity," Rachel yelled to Richard as he made his way toward the choir.

Joyce was excited. "Rachel, what do you think?"

"Yeah, from what I'm hearing, I think I'm going to like this gig. So call me tomorrow and give me all the details." Rachel replied with eagerness.

"Okay meet me back here at 6pm next Wednesday. And as I said, get ready to go on the journey of your lifetime."

CHAPTER 41

Joyce was correct in her assumptions. Since joining the choir and becoming Joyce's assistant, Rachel was having the time of her life. She had the opportunity to travel to different cities to perform and meet famous celebrities as well. The choir was so popular that a well-known producer wanted them to make a CD. Richard was very pleased with this opportunity and began preparing the choir for its first studio session.

The CD was a success and in an effort to promote it, the choir had to go on tour. Unfortunately, this would not be an event that Rachel would be a part of. The date of her wedding had been set long before she became a member of the choir.

Richard was extremely disappointed that Rachel could not accompany the choir on its big debut. For some odd reason, he had developed strange feelings toward Rachel, and each time he saw her at choir rehearsal, these feelings would grow stronger. He could not explain what was happening and tried to shake these feelings off, because, after all, in a few months Rachel would be a married woman. He never mentioned his feelings concerning Rachel to anyone, and God forbid if he showed any interest toward her in public. Richard realized that the sensible thing to do was to keep his emotions hidden, and suppressed within his heart. On the day the choir returned to Dallas, Rachel was having rehearsals at the church where her wedding was to take place the

The Seventh Wife

following day. The moment Richard's plane landed, he quickly rushed out the airport terminal, hopped into a cab, and headed to the church. When he arrived at the church, he frantically began looking for Rachel.

"Sir can I help you?" the security guard asked.

"Yes, I'm looking for Ms. Rachel Tatum I believe she's having rehearsals here for her wedding," Richard spoke with excitement.

"Yes she's here, but is she expecting you?" the guard asked with curiosity.

"No, but… I just need to speak with her for just a second," Richard stated eagerly as he continued walking.

"Sir! If you would just hold up, I'll see if I can find her for you. Please have a seat out in the lobby!" the guard demanded. "What's your name?"

"Richard McWilliams or you can tell her it's Brother Richard."

"Okay, like I said, wait here."

Richard had no choice except to obey the wishes of the guard. After all, he did not want to do anything to mess up his chance to see Rachel.

The security guard found Rachel alone with three other women in a room trying on her wedding dress. His knock on the door was not well received by the women. "Who is it?" Rachel yelled with anger.

"It's Raymond, the security guard sorry to bother y'all but there is a man out here who wants to see Ms. Rachel."

"What's his name?" Rachel yelled.

"He said his name was Brother Richard."

Rachel was surprised by the guard's reply and opened the door to look at him face to face to make sure she heard him correctly. "Did you say, Brother Richard?" she asked in a surprised tone.

"Yes ma'am he first said his name was Richard McWilliams, and then he said you would know him by the name of Brother Richard."

"Who is Brother Richard?" Cousin Sandra asked with curiosity.

"He's the man who started the choir I sing with."

"Okay...but what is he doing here?" she asked again in curiosity.

"I don't know." Rachel was curious.

"Do you want me to get rid of him?" Cousin Sandra asked.

"No, I'll go out to see what he wants because if I don't, he won't leave. He's one persistent man. Okay, Mr. Raymond, I'll step out into the hall way, and then you can bring him back here."

When Richard laid eyes on Rachel, he was blown away by her appearance. For a brief moment, he stood and gasped with astonishment, unaware that Rachel was speaking to him.

"Brother Richard, what are you doing here?"

Rachel asked with an inquisitive tone.

"Rachel...you look amazing," Richard's words finally stumbled out of his mouth slowly.

"Thank you, but you didn't answer my question, what are you doing here?"

"I just really needed to see you," Richard murmured with emotion.

"Why? Why did you need to see me?" Rachel inquired in confusion.

"I...don't know I just wanted to say..."

"Say what? Richard what's going on?" Rachel was losing her patience with Richard.

"I just wanted to tell you good luck tomorrow, and if your man doesn't know it, he is one lucky guy."

"Thank you Brother Richard but I've got rehearsals, and standing out here talking to you is putting me behind schedule. Goodbye," Rachel remarked in a rude tone.

Richard stood there for a moment and watched as Rachel disappeared from sight. After seeing her in her wedding dress, he now had a better understanding of his emotions. "I love her. That's it... I have fallen in love with this woman," he murmured to himself. "And there's nothing I can do about it because she's getting married tomorrow!"

Richard frowned and shook his head in frustration. He took a long, deep breath and left the church realizing that this time, his heart's desires would not be fulfilled by a woman.

CHAPTER 42

Three years later

Rachel was a great mom. Her favorite enjoyment was getting up on Saturday mornings to prepare breakfast for her children. To get her morning started she kept a small radio in the kitchen. She turned the volume up to her favorite gospel station, KHGR and began singing along with a song. In fact, she was singing so loud that she didn't hear the phone ringing and was startled, when her daughter April tapped her on the shoulder to give her the phone. "April, you scared the hell out of me!"

"Mom, you have a phone call and if you would turn the radio down you could hear the phone!"

"Sorry baby. Hello?"

"Rachel, this is your old friend Joyce."

In disbelief, Rachel stool still for a moment then continued her conversation with a surprise scream. "Joyce from the choir?"

Joyce chattered away as if time had never passed between her and Rachel. "Yes, the one and only. Rachel you're not going to believe this but I found your number in an old purse I was giving away to a thrift store, and I decided to call to see if you still had the same number."

"Yes as you can see, it's still the same."

"You know I have missed you over the years. After you got married, you just kicked me and the choir to the curb," Joyce replied playfully.

"I know. It was nothing personal I just wanted to devote my time to my husband and my kids."

The Seventh Wife

"I understand. So…how's your hubby and the kids?" Joyce asked, probing for information.

"The kids are great, but I don't know how William is doing because we're divorced."

For a brief moment, there was silence on the phone after Rachel dropped the bomb on Joyce. "What? Did I hear you say that you and William are divorced?" she inquired with shock.

"Yep, that is what I said," Rachel replied with confirmation.

"When did this happen?" Joyce asked in surprise.

"Last year things began coming unraveled. I was miserable, he was miserable, the kids were miserable. So somebody had to get off the merry-go-round. I moved out, rented me and the kids an apartment, and filed for divorce."

"Wow, I'm sorry to hear that it didn't work out for you and William because I know how much you loved him."

"Don't be sorry Joyce, I'm fine. I am happy, the kids are happy and we're doing great. So, enough about me how are you doing?"

"Things are going great. I'm still in the choir, and I'm still working for Brother Richard."

"That's great."

"Hey what are you doing Friday night at 7?"

"At this moment, I don't think I have anything on my agenda. What's going on?"

"Well, you know our radio station won a stellar award this year, right?"

"Yes, I heard one of the DJ's announcing it the other day, that's awesome."

"To celebrate, Brother Richard is throwing a party at the radio station and he is requesting the attandance of all choir members, a few pastors who broadcast on the radio and some of our listening audience. Who knows? We might have Shirley Cesar, or Yolonda Adams walking up in here. Please say you'll attend, I would love to see you."

"Okay, I'll be there. Thanks for inviting me. I will see you Friday at seven."

The moment Rachel walked into the room on Friday night, Richard spotted her. Briskly, he made his way over to her. "Rachel, how nice to see you."

"Richard, how are you?"

"Great now that you're here. Could I get you something to drink, or something to eat?" Richard was enchanted by Rachel and his actions were of those of a nervous school boy who was finally getting the opportunity to meet the girl of his dreams.

"No, I'm good, I'm just going to mingle for a while, and maybe later on I'll grab a bite to eat." Rachel began to walk away because Richard was getting on her nerves. At that moment, she saw Joyce approaching.

"Rachel thanks for coming and you look so good!" Joyce yelled with excitement. "I see you've already been tackled by Brother Richard."

"Yes, he literally tackled me the moment he saw me he started hugging me so closely I could barely breathe! Joyce, what's up with that man anyway?"

"You really don't get it do you?" Joyce replied.

"No, get what?" Rachel was becoming annoyed by Joyce.

"Rachel! That man is crazy about you?" Rachel shouted with surprise. "What! Come on, you can't be serious!"

"Yep, I'm serious Richard has been carrying a torch for you for three years."

"Are you serious? He's never said anything to me about this… torch."

"Rachel, he's in love with you. I know this for a fact because one day I overheard him talking on the phone to his mother about you. However, since you were a married woman, he never approached you about his feelings. All these years, he has suppressed his love for you and gone on with his life."

Rachel refused to believe what Joyce told her. Not that it mattered anyway if Richard had feelings for her because she had no interest in him at all. In fact, if he was the last man on earth, she still would not have any feelings for him.

"So, what are you going to do?" Joyce asked curiously.

Rachel was annoyed by Joyce's question. "Do about what?"

"Brother Richard! I mean, you're single, he's single…I think you two would make a cute little couple."

"Joyce I don't like Brother Richard. In fact, I can't stand him! He's loud, arrogant, he's not handsome at all and there is no way I would ever consider dating him!"

"Wow! You're serious aren't you?" Joyce replied in surprise.

"Yes I'm really serious! Is this why you invited me to this party, so I could hook up with Brother Richard?" Rachel's expression was one of anger. "Did he tell you to invite me?"

"No Rachel that is not the reason I asked you to come to the party. I thought you would enjoy seeing some of the old choir members. Brother Richard didn't know you were coming to the party."

"Well, it doesn't matter because I'm leaving! Thank you for inviting me and I hope your party is a great success."

"Rachel, please don't leave!" Joyce pleaded with Rachel as she made her way from the radio station. When Joyce returned to the party, Richard approached her."

"Have you seen Rachel?" he inquired excitedly.

"There are so many people here I've lost sight of her."

Joyce began walking away without replying to Richard and that's when he grabbed her hand. "Joyce, have you seen Rachel?"

"She left." Joyce replied in a stern tone.

"What do you mean she left?" Richard asked with weariness reflected on his face.

"Brother Richard, she's gone. She got upset with me and she left."

"Why was she upset?" he asked in concern.

Joyce was somewhat reluctant to reply to Richard but she knew if she did not reply, he was not going to let it go. "I told her the truth, that you were in love with her," Joyce replied.

"Why would that upset her?" Richard asked.

Joyce did not reply to Richard's question, instead, she turned and began walking away. Once again, Richard took hold of her arm, but immediately he let go when he felt her arm stiffen. "Joyce, I'm sorry," Richard stated in an apologetic tone. "I'm just puzzled as to why Rachel would get upset after you told her that I loved her."

"She doesn't like you Brother Richard. In fact, she said that if you were the last man on earth, she still would not date you. She got angry with me because she assumed that I was trying to make some sort of love connection between you two. This is why she left. My advice to you is to give it up and focus your attention on someone else."

"I don't want anyone else." Richard replied with determination. "God told me that one day, Rachel was going to be my wife, and I believe Him. I've waited three years for God's promise to come to pass! If I have to wait three, four or five years for her, I'll just have to wait to see what God does! I know that God is a man that cannot lie."

Joyce was speechless and stared at Richard with disbelief. "You're serious...aren't you?"

"Yes, I love Rachel and I'm not going to give up until she's my wife," Richard replied with certainty.

"You are unbelievable. Love is staring you in the face, and you're chasing after the affections of a woman who does not give a damn about you! Truly unbelievable," Joyce murmured these words as she walked out the room leaving Richard perplexed in his thoughts.

CHAPTER 43

Rachel's mother had been hospitalized for dehydration and her daughter, April, suggested that everyone should plan a trip to Arkansas to visit her grandmother. Rachel made the arrangements and everyone left for Arkansas Saturday morning. Her mother was overjoyed to see Rachel and her grandchildren.

Three days later, at 5 a.m. Rachel woke up in a panic from an unusual dream that someone was speaking to her concerning her mother. Surely, dehydration was not a serious medical condition, but in her dream, she distinctly heard a voice saying that God was going to take her mother home.

The voice also told her to go to Arkansas and take her father, who was in a nursing home, to see his wife for the last time. Disturbed by her dream, Rachel called her friend Joyce for comfort, and Joyce informed Rachel that perhaps she had heard the voice of the Holy Spirit, and she should be obedient to the voice, otherwise she would live in regret if her mother did pass away.

Without hesitation, Rachel contacted her job and requested time off, and made preparations to go to Arkansas. Three hours later, she arrived at the nursing home, retrieved her father, and proceeded to the hospital. Arriving at the hospital, she was greeted by her sister Eloisa who told her that the doctor had given their mother a one percent change to recover from her illness.

Rushing to her mother's bedside, anguish and sorrow consumed Rachel's heart as she gazed into the loving face of her dear sweet mother. "Mommy, I'm here and it's going to be okay…I love you mommy." Rachel struggled to keep her voice calm, but it quivered with sorrow.

"Rachel, mother can't speak," Eloisa replied sorrowfully. "She hasn't spoken a word for days now. In fact, your name was her final word before she lost her voice…"

The thought of not being able to hear final words from her mother consumed Rachel with sorrow and tears began to fill her eyes. She knew she had to be the rock in the family to hold things together. With a tiresome reaction, she wiped her tears and managed to make a request that her mother would have wanted. "Has a pastor been here to pray for mom?" she asked her sister.

"No, I'm sorry it didn't cross my mind to contact a pastor," Eloisa replied, choking back tears.

"I understand Sis I'll take care of it." Rachel walked out the room, went to the nurse's station, and asked the nurse if she could contact a local pastor to come to the hospital to pray for her mom. Within the hour, two pastors were at the hospital saying prayers over her mother.

At 5:45pm, the phone rang and Rachel picked up the receiver. "Hello, this is Rachel."

"Rachel, this is Brother Richard, I'm sorry to call you at this inopportune time, but Joyce has just informed me about your mother's condition, and if you don't mind, I would like to pray with you for a moment." Richards's voice was soothing and sincere.

Rachel was shocked by the unexpected phone call from Brother Richard, but she did welcome his thoughtfulness and allowed him to pray for her. "That will be fine," she replied in a somber tone. Brother Richard's prayer was encouraging and calming to Rachel's heart and he ended his prayer with a profound statement that Rachel would need in order to perform the task ahead. His last words were, "I pray God will give you the strength and grace to face the dark days head." After his prayer, Rachel felt a sense of strength rushing through her mind.

Sadly, within minutes of hanging up the phone, Rachel's mother passed away. Gazing around the room, glaring at the emotional sorrow on the faces of her siblings and her father, Rachel knew that each of them were too distraught to make the necessary arrangements for her mother.

After the doctors took care of the necessary details, Rachel made the arrangements of calling the funeral home, and completed the details with the hospital. This was one of the saddest days of Rachel's life and she prayed to God that the familiar saying that "time will heal all wounds" would be true one day soon.

CHAPTER 44

After returning to Dallas, Rachel called the radio station to thank Richard for his prayers, and for the flowers he and the choir had sent for her mother's funeral.

When Joyce answered the phone, she was excited to hear Rachel's voice. "Rachel how are you?"

"I'm okay, but you know my mom and I were really close, and I'm definitely going to miss my mama. Joyce I know you are busy and I really called to speak to Brother Richard, I would like to thank him for his kindness towards my family and me. Is he there?"

"Yes, he's here, I'll ring his office." Joyce was excited to the point that she could barely transfer the call to Richard. "Brother Richard, you won't believe who's on the phone," she stated with exhilaration.

"Joyce, calm down and tell me who's on the phone!"

"Rachel Tatum is on the phone!" she shouted with enthusiasm.

"Well put her through!" Richard replied with excitement. "Rachel, to what do I owe this pleasure?"

"Brother Richard, I just wanted to call and thank you for your kindness and your prayers. I know you are a busy man, yet you took the time out of your busy schedule to contact me when I was in Arkansas. So, I am so grateful for your kind gesture."

"Rachel you're welcome and if there's anything I can do for you, please don't hesitate to contact me."

"Thanks Brother Richard, you have a great day." Rachel expressed her gratitude and hung up.

Richard's expectation was to continue his conversation with Rachel but was disappointed when she abruptly ended the call.

Immediately, Joyce ran into Richard's office displaying a big smile of hope. "What did she say? Are you taking her out on a date?"

"Joyce please stop! No, I am not taking her on a date. She just called to thank me for my kindness when her mother passed away."

"Oh." Joyce murmured with disappointment.

"Personally, I think you are wasting your time. As I said before you don't know when love is staring you right in the face," Joyce remarked in a condescending tone as she proceeded out the door. However, this time, her remarks did not go unnoticed and Richard confronted her.

"So you're saying that I'm chasing after the affections of Rachel when I should accept the fact that you are in love with me?" Walking towards the door Joyce paused and stood still in her tracks. Then slowly she turned around to face Richard. "Are you in love with me Joyce?" Richard asked curiously.

"Yes. I've been in love with you for a long time and it's obvious that you don't have any idea or don't care how I really feel about you!" Joyce became emotional and tears began streaming down her face.

Richard walked over and held Joyce's hand. Desperate for his affection provoked Joyce to react on a sudden impulse, and she planted a passionate kiss on Richard's lips. Her shocking action caught Richard off guard, and he had to free himself from her embrace. "Joyce, no! Please understand, I do love you but you are like a sister to me, so don't ever do that again! Do you understand?" he asked firmly.

Joyce was embarrassed by her action and could not look Richard in the face. "Yes, I understand. But, if you're so set on dating Rachel, you had better step up your game before someone else beats you to the punch." Joyce left the room with a broken heart, yet she had received confirmation that there was no way Richard would ever fall in love with her.

CHAPTER 45

After Joyce left Richard's office, the remark she made concerning Rachel continued to eat away at Richard's mind. What exactly did she mean when she said, "You had better step up your game, before someone else beats you to the punch?" Richard knew in his heart that since his first wife Carol, he had never had feelings for a woman like the ones he had for Rachel and he knew whatever it took, one day she would be his wife. He knew that if this was ever going to become a reality, he had to do something to gain Rachel's affections.

Immediately Richard emerged from his office to ask Joyce to explain the remarks she had made concerning Rachel. "Just FYI, I saw Rachel and William leaving a restaurant a few days ago."

"Who is William?" Richard asked in confusion.

"William is Rachel's ex-husband," Joyce replied with a serene gesture.

Richard stood still and a wearisome expression appeared on his face as he shook his head in anguish. "Her ex-husband? Is she dating her ex-husband?"

"I don't think so she would have told me that she was dating him. I mean, after all, I am her best friend."

"Joyce since you're Rachel's friend, could you talk to her for me? You've known me for a long time and you know that I am a good man. All I want to do is take Rachel out to dinner and spend some time with her so she can get to know me. Could you do this for me, please?" Richard was pleading to Joyce with his whole heart.

Joyce fell into her chair, leaned back, and sighed in frustration. Glaring up into Richard's pain stricken face, she was puzzled as to how it was possible for this man to be so in love with someone he had never kissed, or had any sexual contact. Could it be possible that God had told him that Rachel was going to be his wife? She had no idea, but since he was so determined to marry Rachel, and because of the love she had for Richard, his happiness was important to her. This left her with only one option and that was to help him win the affections of Rachel. "Yes, Brother Richard, I'll call her and I'll talk to her on your behalf."

Jubilation erupted from Richard and he picked Joyce up and hugged her. "Thank you Joyce, hey lunch is on me." Reaching into his pocket, he pulled out a twenty-dollar bill and placed it into Joyce's hand.

"Thank you, so can I go to lunch now?" Joyce asked playfully.

"Yes, right after you make that call." Richard demanded. Returning to his office, Richard felt a sense of accomplishment. With the help of Joyce, he had the assurance that soon he would have the long awaited opportunity to connect with Rachel.

In the meantime not wanting to disappoint Richard, Joyce made a phone call to Rachel. "Rachel, this is Joyce."

"Joyce, how are you?"

"I'm fine," she replied happily.

"Are you busy?" Joyce asked quickly.

"No, what's up?"

"I don't want to sound like I'm butting in your business, but the other day I saw you and William coming out of a restaurant, are you two back together?"

"Well as you said, you should stay out of my business, but since you're my friend I guess I can share a few things with you. William and I are not getting back together. He had some papers I had to sign concerning the house."

"Oh thank God!" Joyce shouted with relief. "I thought maybe you guys were trying to reconcile your marriage."

"No sweetheart, you know me, I never back track myself. When it's over, it is over. Anyway, what's on your mind?"

"I wanted to talk to you about Brother Richard."

"Joyce…give me a break… I've already told you that I don't like this man!" Rachel was becoming frustrated with Joyce's persistent gestures concerning Richard. "You know what Joyce, why don't you date Brother Richard? I mean since you're so concerned about his wellbeing," Rachel shouted with anger.

"He doesn't want me, he wants you. I did tell him that I loved him, but he loves you Rachel. He said God told him that you were going to be his wife. Who says things like that? He has said it so many times until I am starting to believe that maybe God did tell him that you are supposed to be his wife. Yes, I love him, but I have decided the least I can do is try to convince you to take advantage of this opportunity. Because if you do not, I personally believe that, you will miss one of the greatest blessings of a lifetime. The way I see it, you have given all those other losers a chance so why not give Brother Richard a chance?"

Rachel was silent for a moment grasping the logic of the last statement that Joyce had made. "Joyce, I wouldn't exactly call my ex-husbands losers."

"I'm sorry, but trust me neither of them could hold a candle to Brother Richard. Rachel just go out on a date with him, and if it turns out to be a disaster, then at least you can say you did give it a shot." Joyce's voice pleaded with Rachel.

With frustration Rachel yelled, "Ok! You're wearing me down! I'll go out with Richard and if there's not a slight connection between me and him, I'll tell him not to bother me again."

With excitement Joyce screamed. "Wonderful! So, would it be okay if I tell him to call you now?"

"That would be fine tell him to give me a call because I know he's probably sitting by the phone waiting for your reply."

Rachel was correct in her assumption because five seconds after Joyce got off the phone with her, Richard called, excited to the point that it appeared that he was stuttering the moment he heard her voice. He didn't tell her where their first date would be. He informed Rachel that once everything was arranged he would contact her with the details.

Little did Rachel know but her life was about to be propelled into a fascinating adventure.

CHAPTER 46

Two days later, Rachel was at home preparing dinner when she received a phone call from Richard's secretary. "Hi Rachel this is Joyce, sorry to bother you but I wanted to know if you have plans for Saturday afternoon say about 2 pm?"

Putting down a hot cookie sheet she had just taken out of the oven, Rachel replied to Joyce's question. "No, I'm free on Saturday."

"Great, I will pick you up at about 1:15pm," Joyce replied hurriedly as she was retrieving another call on her phone.

"Joyce, are you still there?" Rachel was still on the line.

"Sweetie, I'm sorry but I've got to answer this other line. I can't tell you where you're going because it's a surprise, just be ready to have some fun! Gotta go!" she shouted with excitement.

Saturday came and Joyce promptly arrived at Rachel's house at 1:15pm. "Joyce, where are we going?" Once again, Rachel inquired.

"Rachel, don't ask me this question again, just sit back and enjoy the ride."

Twenty minutes later, Joyce pulled into the parking lot to a place called, Medieval Times. Peering out the window Rachel's excitement excelled to its highest height. "Oh my goodness, I have always wanted to come to this place!" Rachel shouted with exhilaration.

"I know because every time we're on this freeway, you've always said that one day you would like to come here, so, today is the day," Joyce replied with a happy gesture.

When Rachel and Joyce entered the building, Richard was standing inside with a bundle of happy face balloons, which he presented to Rachel. He told her by accepting his invitation she had made him extremely happy. Of course, his gesture touched Rachel's heart.

Rachel had a wonderful time on her first date with Richard and since it was a success, she made the decision to go on a second date, then a third date and to her disbelief, she and Richard were actually dating. It turned out that Joyce was right all along.

Richard was a good man. A little eccentric, but everyone has flaws. Rachel discovered that they did have a lot in common. He was fun, he loved to travel, and he wine and dined Rachel constantly. But what really touched Rachel's heart was the fact that he always exemplified kindness, not only towards her, but to her children also. This was a plus to Rachel because it was no secret that her children were the most important individuals in her life. She made it clear to Richard, and to every man that she had encountered in her life. God took first place and then her children were second. Everyone else could fall in place taking the third position. At that time, Richard would agree to anything Rachel wanted, just as long as he was in her life.

Six months had passed since Richard and Rachel begin dating and during this time Richard would repeatedly ask Rachel to marry him but as always, her reply would be no.

No one knew what was going on with Rachel. Her children thought Richard would be a great stepfather, her relatives thought he was a good man and so did her friends. So what was the problem that caused Rachel to say no?

What no one knew was that Rachel was dealing with her own personal demons of uncertainty, confusion, and fear. She felt uncertain, because her previous three marriages had ended in divorce, she was concerned that if she married Richard, this marriage would end in divorce as well.

After three failed marriages, Rachel assumed that perhaps she should stay single and break up with Richard so he could be free to find himself a wife. Surely there was someone who really wanted to get married, because as she had noticed, there appeared to be many desperate women searching for a husband. However, she was not in that category.

Richard's constant marriage proposals prompted Rachel to become withdrawn and distant. Days would pass and she would not have any contact with him. She began refusing his phone calls and she did not accept any of his dates.

One afternoon, Joyce called to inform Rachel of the devastating effects that her actions were having on Richard. "Rachel, you're killing him! You're breaking his heart. He's missing work, and canceling important meetings. He has even cancelled two important out of town business trips because he's depressed. I told him, that if he continues neglecting his job, he's going to get fired. Please Rachel just call him!" Joyce was extremely concerned.

"Joyce, I don't want to sound rude, but what he's going through is not my problem." Rachel replied coldly.

"But he's in love with you Rachel doesn't that mean anything to you?" Joyce asked.

"Joyce I think it would best if Richard started dated someone else. I mean, I've been married three times and divorced three times, and I am just afraid that if Richard and I get married, one day we will end up divorced too. Perhaps I am not the right woman for him. Therefore, I'll call him today and tell him that I think it would best if we broke up."

"Rachel please don't break up with him. Just call him and let him know what's going on. Brother Richard is a very understanding man, and I know if you would just talk to him, you will be able to overcome these issues."

Rachel knew Joyce had been right about Richard so far, why not take a chance and launch out into the deep to see if she was correct this time? "Okay, I'll give him a call and I'll discuss everything with him."

"Great. I promise you won't be disappointed," Joyce replied with assurance.

When Rachel contacted Richard, he was at home lying on the sofa watching television. Something he had done for the past two days. Each day, he would force himself to get out of bed only to sit, and stare at the television for hours. He was so depressed because he had not heard from Rachel. When he received her call, weariness was heard in his voice.

"Richard I would like to apologize for not contacting you over the past few days, but I think it's time that I came clean with you concerning what's going on. Could I come over this evening about seven so we could talk?"

"That would be great Rachel. I am so grateful that you called, I'll be here waiting for you." Rachel's phone call gave Richard a new outlook, and just hearing her sweet voice revived his spirits. Richard got off the sofa, turned off the television, took a hot shower, got dressed, and literally paced the floor most of that afternoon experiencing the joyous anticipation of Rachel's arrival.

Finally at 7pm sharp, anxiously peering from his window, Richard saw Rachel's car pull into the driveway. Hurriedly he rushed over and opened the door. Beaming with happiness, he wrapped his arms around Rachel, greeting her with an exhilarating bear hug. "Rachel I am so excited to see you. Please, come in and sit down. Would you like something to drink?" Richard inquired with excitement.

Rachel's stomach quivered with the anticipation of having to discuss her problem with Richard. Letting out a long sigh, she began to speak. "No thank you Richard I just need to talk to you about what's going on. I am uncertain about marrying you because I am afraid that maybe our marriage won't work. I mean, I've been married and divorced three times! So this tells me that something is wrong, and maybe I should just remain single and let you go on and find someone else."

After Rachel had spoken, a brief moment of silence consumed the room. Then Richard took Rachel's trembling frail hands into his and gently kissed the falling tears that had dampened her face and lovingly gazed into her eyes. "Rachel, I love you, and I need you in my life and I don't care if you've been married ten times, I want you to be my wife. As you already know, I've been married six times and if you will give me a chance, you will be my seventh wife. In the Bible, God introduced the number seven as a symbol of completion.

"Rachel, if you will marry me, you will be the last woman I will ever marry, because you and only you are the only woman who can make my life complete. Before God, I promise I will never leave you or forsake you and the only way I will not be in your life is if God takes me home to be with Him. Please say you will marry me," Richard pleaded.

Rachel's face expressed confusion and she excused herself and walked out on the terrace. Sitting quietly alone she tried to find reasons to convince herself why she should marry Richard.

Never in her life had Rachel had a man pour his heart out to her. Then it dawned on her that to a man like Richard, it was essential that he had someone in his life to love, and take care of. On many occasions, she had heard him say, "My existence on this earth doesn't have any meaning if I don't have someone to share my life with."

Rachel had to admit that she did feel extremely special knowing that this incredible intelligent, successful man actually loved her, a little country girl from Arkansas. "Lord how did this happen?" she whispered. "This man could have his choice of any woman yet he loves me."

Then she reflected on a statement that was spoken by her friend Joyce. "You've given all those other losers a chance why not give Richard a chance?" Joyce was right. How could she deny a man who wanted to make her happy? The least she could do was to give him a chance to prove himself. She had always been a risk taker, so why not take a chance on Richard and if it didn't work out then, she could always move on with her life.

After all, she was not getting any younger, and who knows if she would ever have another opportunity such as this one in her lifetime. So she prayed. "God, I will trust you, and if it's your will for me to marry this man, then your will be done. I'll accept Richard's marriage proposal."

Rachel's time spent on the terrace was taking a nerve-wrenching toll on Richard. He had walked back and forth repeatedly and had decided that he would go outside to the terrace and speak to Rachel. But at that moment, he saw her coming inside.

Rachel walked over to Richard and gazing into his eyes, she gave him his answer. "Yes, I'll marry you. So, let's get this party started."

Overjoyed by Rachel's answer, Richard spontaneously picked her up, spinning her around with jubilation. He kissed her with a passion that lingered with pleasure. When he put her down, immediately he rushed from the room. Rachel had no idea where Richard was going. When he returned, he had a small white box in his hand. Then Richard took the traditional position, got down on one knee and once again, he asked Rachel to marry him. After she replied yes again, Richard opened the small box, took out a beautiful diamond engagement ring, and placed it on Rachel's finger.

Staring at the ring with curiosity, Rachel asked a question. "Wow, you were pretty sure of yourself weren't you? I mean you had already purchased the engagement ring?"

"No Rachel, I wasn't sure that you would say yes to my proposal. This is..."

Rachel was infuriated by Richard actions, and didn't allow Richard to complete his sentence. How dare Richard purchase a ring with the assumption that she would marry him. "Richard, I'm a little pissed that you already have an engagement ring!"

"Rachel, sweetheart, let me finish. I didn't buy this engagement ring! This is my mother's ring! And before it was her ring, it was my grandmother's ring. Baby if you don't like the ring, we can go to the jewelry store and pick you out another one, okay?"

Rachel felt so terrible for thinking the worse about Richard and she apologized repeatedly expressing remorse. "Baby, I'm so sorry, I just thought..."

"Baby don't worry about it. Now do you want this ring or not?"

"Of course I want the ring!"

Richard beamed with satisfaction and gazing into Rachel's eyes, he made her a promise. "Thank you Rachel, you have made me the happiest man in the world and I promise you I will always treat you like a queen and I'll take care of you both in life and in death. When I leave this earth, I'll make sure I have everything in place so you will have plenty of money to have anything you need or want. Rachel I love you unconditionally."

After Richard stopped speaking, for some odd reason, an unusual emotional stirring began to take place within Rachel's heart. A stirring that would give her the final confirmation that this was the kind of man she had dreamed about all her life and she thanked God for giving her one more chance at love.

CHAPTER 47

Rachel's marriage to Richard was like a fairy tale. Her wedding gifts from Richard included a new house, a new car, and he surprised her by fulfilling one of her childhood dreams with a trip to Disney Land.

Often times Rachel had to pinch herself to make sure she was actually living such a wonderful life and she thanked God daily for all her blessings, especially for her wonderful husband.

For the next two years, Rachel's fairy tale marriage to Richard continued but abruptly ended when he lost his job at the radio station. It appeared that the attacks in Richard's life was happening all at once when one by one choir members began leaving his choir and eventually the choir was dismantled.

Things continued spiraling down in Richard's life, because Richard's salary was the bulk of the household income, the small unemployment check he received was not enough to pay the bills. This became a serious issue for him and Rachel. Their vehicles were repossessed, their home was on the verge of foreclosure, and to keep afloat they were forced to file bankruptcy three times.

The stress of not having the ability to provide for his wife began to take a toll on Richard and he found himself spiraling out of control both physically and mentally. Because of the stress, he began to lose weight and at one point, he had an issue with his sight and assumed he was going blind. Without health insurance or money, it was difficult for Richard to seek medical attention. One day during a conversation, Rachel asked Richard if perhaps he could seek medical assistance at the VA hospital. After all, he had an honorary discharge from the Army, and for many years, his military information had been stored away collecting dust. Now, perhaps, was the time his military information could be beneficial to help with Richard's health problems.

Rachel's suggestion concerning the VA was a lifesaving idea because after being examined by the doctors, Richard was diagnosed with Type 2 diabetes. Since his condition had been neglected for many years, it was at a critical point. He had to take insulin injections and several prescribed medications as well.

While Richard's medical conditions were under control, his financial issues were getting worse. Each day his life was bombarded with phones calls from bill collectors. He became overwhelmed with life and on one occasion, he told Rachel she would be better off if he was dead. This way she could collect the one million dollar life insurance policy he had taken out on himself when they got married.

"Richard, man of God, where is your faith? I know we are going through some hard times right now, but this is not the time for you to start doubting God and giving up is not an option. And for your information, I don't have any empathy for you. So, if you do decide to kill yourself, then you had better make sure that you die, because I will not take on the responsibility of caring for an invalid! "This was Rachel's tough love approach.

Flopping down onto the sofa, Richard glared at Rachel as she made her exit from the living room. He was surprised by Rachel's unexpected statement because he had assumed that she would have empathy for him concerning his suicidal notions. She most definitely proved him wrong and apparently, she was not finished with the conversation. He watched as she turned around and made her way back into the room.

"Richard," Rachel spoke with a compassionate sigh, "Baby I'm so sorry, I didn't mean to sound cruel. Just like you, I'm going through hell too. But, we can't give up we just have to put our heads together and find a solution to our problems. Richard, you gotta find a job because you know my little paycheck is not enough to pay the bills. You're going to have to assess your qualifications and determine what you're qualified to do."

Richard was becoming frustrated and he felt even more helpless and defeated as this conversation with Rachel continued. At this moment, he felt incapable of doing anything because for decades all he had known was radio. Richard's mind was racing with the devastating thought of starting over in the corporate world at fifty-eight years of age. "No one is going to hire me I don't have any skills to do anything!" he yelled with frustration.

"Baby don't worry, I know something good will come out of this. Please don't give up." Rachel didn't finish her conversation because at that moment Richard received a phone call from the realtor that sold them their house. "Richard this is Thelma Jones your realtor. How are you and your lovely wife doing? Are you all still enjoying your beautiful house?"

Putting on a façade, Richard forced himself to lie. "Yes ma'am we're still enjoying the house."

"Great. Look, I called to invite you and your wife to an appreciation banquet that my broker is giving for all the clients that have purchased homes with our district office. The banquet will be next Friday night at seven pm at the Hilton Inn, on 3108 Rosemont Street. Do you think you and Rachel will be able to attend?"

"Let me check with Rachel she's standing right here." Rachel nodded her approval. "Yes Thelma, we'll be there."

"Great, I'll see you then. Ya'll have a great day, goodbye," Thelma said with excitement.

"Do you really want to go to some dull banquet?" Richard asked with exasperation. "I'm not in the mood to go anywhere."

"Yes, I really want to go, because who knows, you might meet someone there who could give you some leads about a job," Rachel pointed out with concern.

Richard knew he had no choice in the matter because if Rachel said they were going, then it was a done deal. "Rachel, you might be right maybe someone at the banquet could give me a lead on a job, God knows I'll accept anything right about now."

CHAPTER 48

Running late, Richard and Rachel quietly took their seats in the back of the room and it was no accident that they arrived only moments before the speaker, Roger Davis, was making his opening remarks. "Ten years ago, after working for the Dallas police department for twenty-five years, I unexpectedly found myself unemployed. I was fifty-eight years old and, I have no idea how I was going to support my family. I had a two thousand dollar mortgage payment, day care payments, utility bills and two car notes. I was overwhelmed with credit card debt and so on.

My back was up against the wall and I was living a nightmare and I had nowhere to turn, because for twenty-five years, I had been a police officer and I didn't consider myself as being qualified to do anything else."

At that moment, Richard and Rachel gazed at each other in amazement because what Mr. Davis was saying was exactly the same scenario that they were going through. "See Richard, I knew there would be a blessing for us if we came to the banquet," Rachel murmured in a quiet voice.

"Rachel be quiet. I don't want to miss anything." Richard quickly replied.

"So, with my back up against the wall, I asked God to give me a plan in order for me to provide for my family. Fortunately, I had a loving sister, Mrs. Thelma Jones, who knew what I was going through, and she suggested that I should enroll in real-estate school to become a realtor. Now, I have to admit, that I was terrified to step out the box and try something new, but as I said my back was up against the wall, and I had to provide for my family so I was willing to try almost anything if it was honest to provide for my family.

I went to real-estate school, got my license, and started working for the first broker who would take a chance on me. With hard work, I became a multimillion-dollar top realtor within six months. This continued for five years, and then I went back to school, got my broker's license, because I was tired of my broker getting a lump sum of money that I had worked so hard to earn.

Then I took it a little further and applied for a position as a manager at Fannie Mae. I got that position, then I climbed up the ladder a little higher, and as I speak, I am now the vice president at Fannie Mae for the North Texas region."

Thunderous applauds echoed throughout the room, as Roger finished speaking.

"That's the answer to my problem. I know how to sell, so I could become a realtor. Rachel, this was a divine set up by God to arrange for us to be here to hear this man's encouraging testimony." Richard's voice was filled with excitement.

"As I close, I want to encourage individuals to keep moving forward, keep trusting God, because when one door closes, God will always open another one. He will open doors and bless you better than the ones that closed on you. God bless you all and if there's anyone who would like to speak to me after the banquet, please feel free to do so."

After the banquet, Richard had the opportunity to speak to Mr. Davis, and he eagerly thanked him for the encouraging words of hope that he had seeded into his life. He also met with Mrs. Jones and discussed the possibilities of him becoming a realtor. She encouraged him to drop by her office the following week and she would provide the information for the real estate school.

Richard left the banquet with a renewed outlook on life. Stirring within, he felt the confidence that he was accustomed to once again rising to a renewed height.

When he and Rachel were seated in the car, Richard leaned over and gently took Rachel's face in his hand and planted a big juicy kiss on her soft lips.

Rachel asked playfully. "What was that for?"

"Rachel McWilliams, I love you so much. Had it not been for your encouragement to go to this banquet, I would have missed one of the greatest opportunities of my life. I thank God for you every day. In the Bible, there is a scripture that says, "A man who findth a wife finds a good thing." Baby you are definitely my good thing!"

"Thank you, baby, you're my good thing too and if we keep God as the head of our lives, and our house, we'll be okay. Now, let's go get some real food because that junk we had at the banquet looked like rabbit food!" Rachel playfully exclaimed as she and Richard drove off into the moonlit night.

CHAPTER 49

Eight months later, Richard received his real estate license and became a million dollar top seller at his brokerage firm. The money was rolling in and Richard and Rachel were in a financial position to pay off the majority of their debts. Unfortunately their mortgage was too far behind to catch up so they decided that it would be in their best interest to sell their house and on the brink of foreclosure, the house sold. It was heart breaking for Rachel to walk away from her dream house, but she knew that letting go of the old would only make room for the new.

Richard and Rachel decided to rent a house and save their money until their credit improved. Then they would build their dream home. After two years working for his broker, Richard was becoming annoyed and he decided to leave his brokerage firm. He was indecisive concerning his next step and the thought of working for someone completely repulsed Richard. One afternoon Richard shared his thoughts with Rachel.

"Why don't you start your own business?" she suggested.

Suddenly a ray of hope shined in Richards's eyes. "Baby you're a genius!" He shouted with joy. "I can do this I can start a property management company. But I'll need to find investors, who will let me manage their properties, and I can still be a realtor. I just need a broker to transact my closings when I sell a house!" Richard was extremely excited. "Later on, once I'm established in my business, maybe I'll go back to school to get my broker's license, and I won't have to split my money with no body," Richard said with assurance.

Rachel knew how importance it was for Richard to accomplish his goals. Therefore, she borrowed five thousand dollars from her bank to assist him with his efforts to acquire office space and equipment for his business. Within two months, RLM Properties was open for business and because of Richard's tenacious work ethics, within weeks of opening he had acquired five investors and twenty-five different properties to manage. Business was booming so Richard decided to hire a staff to maintain his workloads. At that time, hiring a staff appeared to be an exceptional idea that is until his staff started taking advantage of his generosity and his office became somewhat of a social gathering rather than a business environment.

On one occasion, Richard's office was burglarized and his entire phone system was stolen. With the assumption that perhaps his employees were involved in the burglary, and not wanting to point the finger at anyone, Richard decided to disband his staff and go solo with the assistance of Rachel. Rachel suggested in order to save money it would be wise to transfer the office into their home. Richard agreed and from then on, their business would be operated from the comfort of their house.

As the years passed, Richard and Rachel began to do a lot of traveling. There were cruises to the Bahamas, Mexico, and the dream trip of a lifetime was to Tokyo, Japan. Yes, life was good for Rachel and Richard but only for a few years. Once again, death was about to make a horrific impact in Richard's life.

Early one Friday morning in May, Richard received a heart-wrenching phone call from his eldest daughter, Lesley. Lesley informed her dad that his mother was hospitalized and she was in critical condition suffering from pneumonia.

Immediately Richard began preparing to make the trip to Ohio to be with his mother. Unfortunately, he didn't make it in time because a few hours later he received another phone call from his daughter informing him that his mother had passed away. Devastated and distraught about the loss of his mother, Richard helplessly fell to his knees and wept uncontrollably for over an hour.

There was no comforting Richard even Rachel's presence could not console the hurting space within Richard's heart. Tightly holding Richard's trembling body Rachel assured him that she was there for him. "Baby I'm here and it's going to be okay, just cling to me and we'll get through this together." Having lost her mother a few years prior, Rachel could relate to the sorrow that Richard was experiencing.

Finally, later in the day, Rachel managed to calm Richard to a point to where he could call his daughter. "Lesley, this is daddy, I 'm so sorry it's taken me so long to return your call but I was just blown away when you told me that mama had passed," Richard spoke with a sorrowful tone.

"Daddy I understand," Lesley replied and a faint tone of despair could be heard in her voice. "Daddy since grandmother is gone there is no need for you to rush up here. Selena and I are the beneficiaries of grandmother's insurance policies so we can make all the funeral arrangements and we will contact you if we need anything. After the funeral arrangements are made, we'll contact you with the information. I know you're trying to run your business and we'll be fine."

"Lesley are you sure you and Selena can handle everything?"

"Yes daddy, Selena and I aren't little girls anymore. We will be fine. Trust me we're capable of taking care of grandmother's funeral." Lesley sounded confident.

"Thank you Lesley, tell Selena I so appreciate everything you girls are doing. Lesley, if you need anything, please call me. Whenever you call back, I'll book our flights and we will rent a car at the airport and drive to the house."

"Okay Daddy, I'll talk to you later. Love you."

It saddened Richard knowing that going to Ohio would never be the same. Never again would he have the opportunity to see his sweet mother's face. Never again would he have the opportunity to hear her sweet voice. His thoughts got the best of him, as tears started gushing from his eyes. Unable to conceal the pain and sorrow that was tearing his heart apart, Richard released an agonizing scream that echoed throughout the room. "Mama!"

CHAPTER 50

It rained the day of the funeral and the outdoor burial procedures did not take place until the following day. After the pink flowered casket was lowered into the grave, for almost thirty minutes, Richard stood alone at the gravesite. Patiently, Rachel and Richard's daughters had waited in the car, but Richard had not moved from the gravesite. "Girls sit tight it's starting to rain again so I'm going to get your dad," Rachel stated with a compassionate tone.

When Rachel approached Richard, she could hear him murmuring to himself. Quietly she stood back in the distance, giving him a moment of privacy. After Richard finished speaking he glanced in Rachel's direction, walked over, and embraced her. A smile of peace lingered on his face. "I'm okay. I just wanted to say my final goodbyes to mama. Are you okay?" Richard asked with concern.

"Yes, I'm fine I'm just concerned about you."

Richard grabbed Rachel's hand and began running towards the car. "Come on let's get out of the rain."

When Richard returned to the car, his daughters were exceedingly concerned about their father's wellbeing. "Daddy are you okay?" both girls asked at the same time.

Reaching for the hands of his daughters, Richard affectionately assured them that he was fine.

In addition, he thanked them for taking care of the funeral arrangements for their grandmother. "Everything was lovely and I am so proud of you both. I'll be here a few more days to help out with any loose ends concerning mama's house, or her bills. Just let me know what I can do to help my babies out, okay?"

"Thank you daddy, but seriously, Selena and I have everything under control and after the reading of the Will is done, I don't think there will be any need for you to stick around. And I know you're itching to return to Dallas to take care of your business, right?" Lesley's words were to the point.

"Mama had a Will?" Richard inquired with surprise.

"Yes, grandmother had a will and the attorney will come by the house tomorrow at ten o'clock to read it. So, make sure that you and Rachel are on time."

The next morning, Mr. Ross, the attorney, arrived promptly at ten o'clock to read the will. The house was left to Lesley and Selena. Both girls received a substantial amount of insurance benefits, so did Richard's son, Richard Jr. Richard and his sibling received ten thousand dollars each from their mother.

After the reading of the will, Richard and Rachel took his daughter's out to dinner. They said their goodbyes to the girls before he and Rachel drove to the airport.

A few weeks after his mother's death, Richard received proceeds from his mother's insurance company. Richard used these funds as a down payment on a house. It was not their dream house but he and Rachel were content with their choice.

CHAPTER 51

For over sixteen years, Rachel and Richard had been in love but something strange was taking place in their relationship. It was as if an unusual sprit has taken over their hearts and was pulling them further apart each day. Rachel could feel the passion of her husband drifting away but she didn't know how to repair the brokenness that was taking place. She noticed Richard's odd behavior after he starting receiving peculiar phone calls at unusual times at night.

Whenever his phone would ring, he would go into the next room to answer the call. Rachel became suspicious and one night when he answered this out of the ordinary phone call, she decided to eavesdrop on the conversation. That's when she overheard Richard speak the name Ellen.

Rachel knew Ellen had been Richard's sixth wife. After all these years, why would she call Richard? Rachel did not tell Richard that she overheard his conversation she just kept it to herself. But a few weeks after his conversation with Ellen, Richard informed Rachel that he had to make a trip to South Carolina.

Rachel was perplexed because she didn't know anyone who lived in South Carolina." Richard, who lives in South Carolina?"

"My stepson, Jackson lives in South Carolina. His mother, my ex-wife, called and said that Jackson was having some issues that maybe I could help him with."

The Seventh Wife

Rachel was extremely curious, so she continued her conversation with a condescending attitude. "Is that right? So, why didn't Jackson call you himself?"

"I don't know! I just know that if my son needs me, then I have to go see what I can do for him." "Richard, is there something going on that you should discuss with me?"

"No, do you have a problem with me going to visit my son?" Richard shouted with anger.

"No, but if you see your son, I'm sure that you're going to see his mother as well! Does she live in South Carolina also?"

"Yes, she moved there after we divorced."

Now, Rachel was extremely frustrated and angry with Richard's plans to go to South Carolina. It was not that she didn't trust Richard, but it was the fact that he did not discuss the matter with her. Rachel felt that Richard had totally neglected her feelings and by doing so, he had made a bold statement that going to South Carolina was his main priority.

Not desiring to cause an explosive argument, Rachel backed off and ended the conversation. She told Richard to have a safe trip and she immediately left the room.

Richard had been in South Carolina for three days and one night, unexpectedly, Rachel received a phone call from her younger sister, who lived in Arkansas. Her sister gave her a prophecy concerning Richard. She told Rachel that the following year, she and Richard would not be married.

Rachel could not believe what she was hearing, but she did take heed to the conversation she had with her sister. When Richard returned home from his trip, Rachel noticed a drastic change in his personality. He became rude, unloving, and critical of almost everything she did. While on a trip at her class reunion, he was rude to her classmates, and at one point, he had the audacity to call her stupid!

Yes, something was terribly wrong with Richard McWilliams and Rachel was beginning to believe that perhaps when he went to South Carolina, someone had placed a voodoo spell on him. Whatever the case, she had decided to just sit back, and wait to see what was going to happen next.

CHAPTER 52

Then it happened that following year, on May 14. Rachel had prepared dinner and was sitting at the table watching her favorite television show when Richard came in and told her that he needed to discuss something with her. Immediately Rachel turned down the volume on the television because from the tone of Richard's voice, this was going to be an extremely important conversation.

Rachel turned and faced Richard. "Rachel, I'm not happy and I want a divorce. I will be moving out of the house." His voice was firm and to the point and after he finished, he immediately turned and walked away and sat motionless on the sofa.

For a brief moment, Rachel remained seated at the table to gather her thoughts. Then she stood up and walked into the room where Richard sat. "Richard, if our season is up, then it's up." No other words were spoken and Rachel went back to the table and continued eating her dinner.

Then Rachel overheard Richard talking on the phone to someone. "She didn't appear to be upset." Richard was puzzled by her reaction to his request for a divorce. Richard did not know that Rachel had already been pre-warned in a prophecy given by her sister.

One week later after Richard informed Rachel about his wishes for a divorce Rachel came home from work and found her divorce papers lying on her bed. "You can sign the papers and I will return them to my attorney," Richard's voice was cold and callous when he spoke.

Rachel did not respond to Richard but she took the divorce papers, read each page, and decided that perhaps it would be sensible to acquire her own attorney to review the decree.

The first court date was set for June, and Rachel did not have any idea who she was going to get to represent her. She grabbed the local directory and chose the first female attorney listed. She chose a woman thinking that she would have empathy concerning her situation. However, Rachel would late discover that this was not the case. Her attorney was all about the money and did not fairly represent her when it was time to go to court.

Rachel was extremely disappointed with the way her attorney was handing her case, so she fired her attorney, and was on the hunt for someone else to represent her for the final hearing. Fortunately, she was able to acquire another attorney to represent her just in time before the next court date, which was in August.

What really was upsetting Rachel was the fact that she had to scrape up money that she did not have, in order to pay for a divorce, that she did not want. She had already paid the first attorney a thousand dollars, now she would be out another thousand dollars or more to pay the second attorney.

The day of the final court date came. Rachel was sitting upstairs awaiting the arrival of her attorney when she was approached by Richard. "Hello Rachel." Richard had this smug smile on his face, a smile that gave Rachel a desire to spit in his face. However, she kept her cool and returned a pleasant reply. "Richard, how are you?" she replied with a fake smile.

"I'm great! I heard that your attorney resigned," he replied in a sarcastic manner.

"Who told you that she resigned?" Rachel was curious to hear Richard's reply.

"Just so happens, that your attorney and my attorney are good friends."

"Really? What a coincidence. But no, she didn't resign, I fired her."

"So I guess that means that you don't have an attorney to represent you. I'm assuming that you probably spent all your money paying your attorney. Right?"

Richard was really trying to slap Rachel in the face with his sarcasm. However, unknown to Richard, Rachel's attorney was standing behind him listening to his attempts to torment Rachel. "Hello Mr. McWilliams." This was the stern voice of Alexis Everson, Rachel's attorney.

Richard's reaction was quick as he turned around to face the person addressing him. Alexis stretched her hand out to shake Richard's hand. "I'm Alexis Everson…Mrs. McWilliams's attorney."

Richard was standing there with egg on his face.

"Mr. McWilliams I would appreciate it if you did not badger my client. Whatever you have to say to Mrs. McWilliams please save it for the hearing." Now directing her attention to Rachel, Alexis requested Rachel to a walk with her so she could discuss a few details before entering the court room.

Twenty minutes into the court proceedings things were not going well for Rachel and her attorney. The main thing Rachel had hoped to acquire in the divorce proceeding was the spousal support to assist with her mortgage payments.

Unfortunately, the Judge denied her request. Rachel's attorney requested that since Rachel has assisted Richard in starting his business she was entitled to receive a percentage of the property management business but this too was denied.

In the conclusion of the trial, the judge did agree to give Rachel ownership of her house. That was great but because Richard's income had been the main source to pay the mortgage, and since he had not given her a dime since moving out of the house in April, the mortgage was over eight thousand dollars in the rear, and her house was on the brink of foreclosure.

After the trial, Richard gazed in Rachel's direction and flashed a devious smile. As Rachel and her attorney made their way out the courtroom, Richard hurriedly caught up with them. Slightly brushing against Rachel he whispered into her ear, "I always win."

A sudden rush of anger overtook Rachel as Richard spoke these hurtful words to her. She managed to keep her cool because there was no way she was going to give Richard the pleasure of seeing her sweat. Instead, in a calm voice, she gave Richard a reply. "Richard, it might appear that you have won round one, but trust me the battle has just begun."

Richard stood there with a confused glare on his face as Rachel and her attorney walked into the elevator.

Once outside the building Rachel's attorney humbly apologized to Rachel for losing her case. "Rachel I am so sorry! If I would have had more time to prepare for your case, I know we would have won. I am so upset! I wanted to nail that arrogant fool to the wall!" Alexis screamed as she slammed her fist against her purse.

"Alexis that's okay don't feel bad, it's going to be fine, at least I have my house, now all I have to do is ask God to show me how to keep my house. God has placed my back so far up against the wall that I have no one else to trust except God. I think the lesson God is trying to teach me is not to trust in a man, because a man will always let you down, but God will never let me down." With a reassuring touch to her attorney's hand, Rachel assured her that in time, everything would work out.

CHAPTER 53

The night after the trial Rachel was extremely restless. Falling to her knees, she began praying. "Father, you are my husband now and I know you will take care of me better than any flesh and blood man can. Just show me what to do and I will follow you." Then suddenly, inside of Rachel's mind, she heard a still small voice ask her a question. "Do you trust me?"

"Yes Lord, I trust you." Rachel got off her knees, went back to bed, and slept peacefully for the remainder of the night.

The next day when Rachel returned to work, her co-workers were anxiously waiting to find out the results of the trial. Immediately they bombarded her with questions. "Did you win?" everyone asked in unison.

"No, I didn't get a dime, but the judge did award me the house." Disappointment was shown on the face of her co-workers. "Apparently I got what God wanted me to have, so I know He's going to give me a plan on how to keep my house, because as I speak, I need eight thousand dollars to prevent my house from going into foreclosure," Rachel replied with exasperation.

After the co-workers dismantled, Rachel's co-worker, Lois, pulled her aside to speak to her privately. "Rachel why don't you contact your mortgage company and see if you would qualify for a modification. If you qualify, they will place the eight thousand dollars at the end of the mortgage and set you up on a new mortgage payment and hopefully your payments will be less than what you are paying now. This is what my husband and I had to do last year."

"Thank you Lois, I'll contact the mortgage company today." Rachel contacted the mortgage company and provided all the documents needed for the modification process and was informed that the modification process would cease any foreclosure procedures. This gave Rachel a sense of ease, yet each evening when she arrived home, she would glance at the front door, looking for a foreclosure notice from the mortgage company.

During this time, while Rachel was waiting to hear from the mortgage company, she received several calls and a few ugly emails from Richard. No matter how hard his attempts were to hurt Rachel, she never gave in or responded to his inquiries. She knew the quickest way to get over someone was to ignore them.

Three months after Rachel applied for a modification she was approved, and her payments were lowered by three hundred dollars. She began to budget her money to take care of her bills and was in the process of acquiring a second job, but her sister and her niece needed a place stay, so Rachel took them in. This was perfect timing because her sister could share the expenses of the house. Rachel was so thankful to God for meeting her needs.

One year after Rachel's divorce, Richard was begging her to forgive him for abandoning her. She stood her ground and informed Richard that it was his decision to leave, and he should move on. Richard refused to take no for an answer and on a continuous basis he made frequent trips by Rachel's house begging her to take him back. Being cautious, Rachel never allowed Richard to enter her home.

Day in and day out the tormenting feelings of regret would consume Richard's mind. He had many weary sleepless nights concerning the terrible decisions he had made. On a constant basis, he would find himself screaming out loudly, "I made a mistake! God I made a mistake!" His screams would go unheard as they echoed throughout the empty house he now lived in alone.

Rachel began getting phone calls frequently from Richard in the early morning hours and late into the night. When she would leave home in the morning to go to work, she would notice Richard's car parked on her street. Rachel was concerned about Richard's unorthodox behavior and had considered contacting the police. However, not wanting to cause any more heartache on Richard, she contacted him and suggested that it would be in his best interest not to call her nor come by her house anymore.

Richard tried one last attempt to patch things up with Rachel. His pleas were of desperation. "Rachel please forgive me. I was a fool to walk out on you, please let me come home. I'm going crazy living in this house alone and I don't see how I'm going to survive without you."

Rachel's reply was firm. "Richard in time, you'll be fine. I wish you the best." With those last words, Rachel hung up the phone.

That night, all the voices from the past consumed Richard's mind. He tossed and turned as he reflected on the voice of his mother, and the voice of his beloved wife Carol. It was as if they were beckoning him from a distance to come with them so he could be at rest. Suddenly in a panic, Richard set up in the bed and began shouting, "Lord I am so tired! I am so tired!"

Peacefully, Richard laid his head down on his pillow and remained there for two days until he was found by his landlord.

CHAPTER 54

Dallas Texas, 2012

"Hello?"

"Hello, is this Mrs. McWilliams?"

"This is Rachel. Who's calling?"

"Mrs. McWilliams, this is Officer Anderson, I'm with the police department. I'm at the home of Mr. Richard McWilliams and I found your number in his cell phone. He had you listed as his wife."

"I am his ex-wife, we were divorced in 2011. Anyway, may I ask why you're calling me?"

"Ma'am I'm calling you because your ex-husband was taken to the VA hospital a few hours ago and the doctors are requesting that family members should come to the hospital immediately. You were the only person that he had listed in his phone as a family member."

With concern Rachel inquired, "Officer Anderson, can you tell me what happen to Mr. McWilliams?"

"At this point we're not sure. The owner of his residence placed the call this morning after he went into the house to do some repairs and he found Mr. McWilliams unconscious lying in his bed. However, I can tell you that it doesn't appear that there was any foul play. Meaning there was not a break in, and it doesn't appear that Mr. McWilliams was injured in any way. I'm sure when you meet with the doctor he will be able to give you additional information."

"Okay. Well, let me make arrangements here at work, and I will head out to the hospital."

"Thank you ma'am, I'm wrapping things up here at the house now and I will meet you at the hospital. I'll be waiting at the entrance to escort you upstairs."

When Rachel arrived at the hospital, Officer Anderson was patiently waiting at the front entrance. "Mrs. McWilliams, please come with me and I'll escort you upstairs to meet with the doctor," he stated quickly with concern.

The doctor was waiting in his office for Mrs. McWilliams. "Officer Anderson, thank you for bring Mrs. McWilliams up."

"Yes sir, I'll just wait outside for you ma'am."

Officer Anderson excused himself and left the office.

"Mrs. McWilliams, I'm Doctor Burns, please have a seat. Mrs. McWilliams, your husband..."

"Doctor Burns, he's my ex-husband."

"It appears that your ex-husband had a stroke, and he is in a semi-conscious state. Meaning, he is drifting in and out of consciousness. He's doing a lot of talking and it appears that he is experiencing a series of flash backs of events that have occurred in his past. However, he is unaware of his immediate surroundings. It's as if he's in his own world. I am sorry to say, and unfortunately, I don't see his condition improving at all. Therefore, if there are any other immediate family members, that you wish to call, I would suggest that you contact them as soon as possible."

"Yes, I'll call his children immediately."

With concern Doctor Burns asked, "Mrs. McWilliams, would you like to see Richard now?"

Rachel spoke with empathy, "Yes, I would like to see him."

"Good, I think your presence would trigger something inside of him that could possibly give him some comfort. As a matter of fact, he has mentioned your name several times."

When Rachel laid eyes on Richard, she was brought to tears. His frail body was attached to tubes plunging in every direction. Rushing over to his side, she gently began rubbing his face with her trembling hands, and never-ending tears started streaming down her face. "Oh Richard my love...I'm here and I won't leave your side. Richard... can you hear me?" she asked in desperation.

Slowly, Richard turned his head and gazed into the tear stained face of his ex-wife and for a brief moment, it looked as if he recognized her, but he didn't. He continued having a conversation with someone who was not in the room. Then he spoke with a weak trembling voice, "Private Barker, I'm so sorry."

Curious, Doctor Burns inquired, "Mrs. McWilliams, who is Private Barker?"

"Doctor Burns, it appears that my dear sweet Richard is taking a journey back down memory lane, and right now he's back in Vietnam. If I remember correctly, Private Barker was a young man who died in an explosion when Richard was in Vietnam."

Sitting in a chair, Rachel positioned herself closer to Richard's bed, and gently took his feeble hand into hers. Rachel always admired his hands. His hands were the first things she noticed about Richard when they first met. They were strong and large, yet so gentle at the same time. "Dr. Burns, if you don't mind I'm going to sit here with my sweetheart for a moment and keep him company while he takes me on the journey of his life, and, oh, what an extraordinary journey Sergeant Richard McWilliams has lived."

Patiently, for hours, Rachel sat with Richard as he tossed and turned fighting with the demons that had consumed his feeble mind. Then suddenly a sense of calmness came over Richard when he turned and saw Rachel sitting next to his bed. Rachel drew nearer to Richard as he tried to speak. "Rachel, you're here. I was just dreaming about you and you're here." Richard's voice was extremely weak. "You were

God's perfect number seven, and I messed up. I love you Rachel, please forgive me," Richard asked with a short panting breath. Then slowly Richard turned his head and gazed upward. Rachel noticed a smile come upon his face and with disbelief she heard Richard's feeble voice murmur "Carol my sweetheart."

Those were Richard's final words as he took his last breath. Immediately, one of the monitors connected to his limp body sounded off with a long screeching sound. Doctors and nurses rushed into the room. He was gone. Finally, the peace that Richard had yearned for had come.

Rachel exhaled a sigh of contentment because she knew no matter what had happened between she and Richard, he would have wanted her to be by his side. Gently Rachel leaned over and kissed Richard on his forehead and quietly murmured, "It is finished my darling, you can rest in peace now. I will all ways love you and one day I will see you again."

Slowly Rachel picked up her purse and walked out the hospital room and called Richard's daughters." Lesley, is your sister there with you? I'm afraid I have some bad news about your dad.

CHAPTER 55

When I learned about Richard's death, my heart grieved for him because he was such a good man. One thing I appreciated about Richard was the fact that he loved Rachel unconditionally. However, the main factor that led to Richard's demise was when he made the unfortunate decision to leave Rachel. Had he known that his actions would be the nail that would seal his own coffin he would have found a way to work things out with Rachel instead of getting a divorce.

After Richard left Rachel and realized he had made a terrible mistake, on numerous occasions he would contact me begging me to call her on his behalf. Yes, I did contact her, but she would not give in. I have known Rachel my entire life and one thing that she has never done is revisit her past. She always said, "If you don't let go of your past, you will miss what God has for your future."

Rachel and I talk to each other every day, and today when she called she was extremely excited. Rachel told me she'd kept a diary since she was a teenager. Today while reading an entry in her diary she made a miraculous discovery. She said, "April, when I was fourteen, I had a horrible nightmare about a family who was involved in a terrible car accident. When I was reading my diary, the Holy Spirit revealed to me that the man in the accident was Richard. It must be true, because Richard did tell me that he and his family were involved in a deadly accident and his wife did die! April, at the age of fourteen, through a dream, I believe God gave me a peek into my future."

"This could be true, I mean, anything is possible with God, right? Therefore, if Rachel's dream was a prophetic sign from God, I personally would say that it was God's plan for Rachel and Richard to be together.

So Richard, rest in peace because Rachel, my mother, would be your last wife, THE SEVENTH WIFE."

April

About the Author

Francile grew up in Magnolia Arkansas. She graduated from Magnolia High School, and moved to Dallas in 1971. Francile is living proof that if you have determination and perseverance, nothing can stop you from accomplishing your dreams and goals. Francile's mother always told her that you are never too old to learn, so at 52 years of age, she enrolled at Dallas Baptist University, and in May 2011 she received a Bachelor's of Arts and Science Degree in Communication.

Francile is the owner of Angel Wing Enterprise. Through her company, she has published six books including her new exciting novel, *The Seventh Wife*.

Books by the Author:

- *How To become a Champion in Life* - A motivational book for teens and young adults
- *Moods and Attitude* - A Christian motivation book for children 3-5 years old
- *The Old Cherry Blossom Tree* - A history book for children 4 and up
- *A Queen for King Laroness* - A fun filled children's book for children 3 and up
- *The Affairs of Love* - An inspirational Christian Novel for women
- *Skeletons. We all have them* - A novel

Francile's main objective is reaching out to hurting people and becoming a positive role model by enhancing, empowering, and educating individuals of all ages. Her motto is, "To be blessed to be a blessing."

CONTACT INFORMATION
Angel Wing Enterprise
P. O. Box 25
Cedar Hill, Texas 75106-0025
Phone: 214-677-8747
Email Address: fmccottry@yahoo.com

www.ingramcontent.com/pod-product-compliance
Lightning Source LLC
LaVergne TN
LVHW051554070426
835507LV00021B/2573